The
bath
full
of
damsons

by

SELINA TROTMAN

With best wishe
Selina Trotman

EDITOR: MIKE WILLMOTT

FRONT COVER: ANGELA THORPE

ART-WORK: MARIANNE KIERNAN

"These were the potters and those that dwelt
among the plants and the hedges."
I Chronicles 4:23

Dedicated to the memory of my parents,
Fred and Alice Farlow,
and of "the children who played".

It is the author's intention that *Prospects for People with Learning Disabilities, PO Box 351, Reading (Charity No.1060571)* of which York House, Bayston Hill is part, will benefit from the profits from sales.

ISBN 0-954305329

PRINTED BY COTON PRINT, WHITEHALL STREET,
SHREWSBURY

CONTENTS

Photograph One – The Family Farlow at *The Thatch*
Photograph Two - Cutting the hay
Introduction

Map
The Farm
Granma Farlow
Wem Baptist Church Ladies Outing to Grinshill (see names on reverse of Donnington School 1937 photo)
Donnington School - 1937
Bishop Street Press – Current Publications

Introduction

A great deal from other people is commemorated in the completion of this book, both in practical help and inspirational encouragement. It was made possible only because of some years exploring the world of adult education with the Workers' Educational Association through Edward Storey at Wedgwood College, Barlaston, but mainly in the Cambridge Branch earlier.

There, the now late Cecil Scrimgeour, as tutor with the Board of Extra-mural Studies, was a powerful influence in thought and discovery in literature, language, and creative writing. His colleague Nicholas Friend was invaluable in his exhortation to - "Now show us the same picture from inside." It was Dr David Rolf of Birmingham University who, with others at the Cambridge Summer School in 1983, confirmed for me that the experiences were worth writing about.

My return to Shropshire set the scene for this writing, helped on its way by kind words from the late Richard Woolley at College Hill House. His successor, Sam Lewellyn, and fellow writers at the Gateway, Shrewsbury, have provided a healthy mixture of praise and tuition in the necessary art of self-criticism for which I am truly grateful.

It was Sam Llewellyn who gave me a verbal push in the direction of Diane Kemp of BBC RADIO SHROPSHIRE. She encouraged me to share the memories with forty broadcasts in 1986. The reaction and encouragement from a number of ex-schoolfellows has given the final spurt to the work's completion.

It has been especially satisfying to find so many of the memories confirmed and conserved in the Shrewsbury Chronicle at the Local Studies Library. It was wonderful to find dates where needed – and particularly proof that the happenings were not mere fragments of my imagination.

Then, just when I needed them, like answer to prayer, along came Kate and Noel Edgar to whom I'm deeply indebted for willingly transcribing my tatty manuscript into acceptable form.

Not least do I thank all members of my patient family. They and I owe our survival to my husband Charles, who has coped with the practicalities of the present day whilst my mind has been pondering the past. Then I met *Bishop Street Press*.

CHAPTER 1

Borrowings

"Last night I dreamt I went to Manderley again."

I have tried to begin this book without borrowing from another, but no other words express my feeling so exactly. For they also began what is to me one of the finest of modern novels, a tale of a place and of its people - and of a mysterious power of relationship. I have read Daphne du Maurier's *Rebecca* a number of times, and have thought of those lines many more. Each time I have sighed, and have felt, "Ah, yes. I know ... I know ..." For who has not dreamt of returning to a place of their moulding?

I left my native Shropshire, not quite looking for gold, yet half prepared not to be surprised if I found it, perhaps on the trees, if not on the pavements, of that then sought-after, south-east of England. Gold there was, but in the western sky, as I gazed watchfully back to the sunset.

At first, I often dreamt of being back in Shrewsbury, searching for silk fabric to buy. I had miraculously unlimited money, and, in those middle nineteen-forties, unlimited clothing coupons, but only five minutes before the shops closed. I can't imagine what an interpreter would make of that.

Later, the dreams came in the form of two pictures, each stimulated by a particular piece of music. Whenever and wherever I heard the opening bars of *The Yeomen of the Guard* a lump in my throat pushed tears down my face, and I felt the soul of me transported. I could smell the roses, the herbs, the moist peat and trodden grass as they can only smell when caught in the heat of a summer afternoon with the crowds under the enormous tarpaulin at **Shrewsbury Flower Show.** I could hear the happy, anxious voices, amid the preponderance of Welsh ones.

"Have you seen Dad yet?"

"Where's Mum? - A prize for his leeks?"

"AND a first for his celery !! ?"

"Here he is!"

Ah, yes! - But occasionally over the years I did go back in person to the **Flower Show.**

The other picture was brought about by a plaintive song. Over the years I heard it, always quite unexpected. Cutting at something too deep for tears, this was a tenor voice, clean and beautiful as a surgeon's blade, singing, '*The Old House*':

"Lonely I wander, through scenes of my childhood.
They bring back the memory of happy days of yore.
Gone are the old folk, the house stands deserted -
No light at the window – no welcome at the door.

Here's where the children played games on the heather,
Here's where they sailed their wee boats on the burn.
Where are they now? Some are dead, some have
wandered.
No more to their homes shall these children return.

Lonely the house now, and lonely the moorland.
The children are scattered, the old folk are gone.
Why stand I here, like a ghost and a shadow:
It's time I was moving – it's time I passed on.

What a song! Each time I have been overcome by a paralysing emptiness, and that feeling of loss which I suppose to be inevitable in sensitive adulthood. And always the picture has been the same - the house, the same one, the large, square, red farmhouse, over the field, at Uckington.

I lived at Uckington, though not in the farmhouse, from 1930 to 1938. It is not that the time was all joy - far from it. Those were years of hardship there, as in the towns; nor do I only remember the joyous parts. But these were the years, and this was the place of my growing. Much that was Uckington came away with me, stuck to me, and is part of me still.

We rarely feel that we are part of the making of history. Events of those times have grown in significance now that we know they were nearing the end of an age. The earlier, industrial, revolution had a limited effect on some parts of the Shropshire countryside. But the changes which were creeping into the mid-thirties and which leapt forth with the approaching war transformed life in hamlet and village, probably even more, proportionately, than in the cities. Each step we trod, every breath we drew, the food we ate - and each song we sang was embryonic history, and yet "we were looking away".

Now, I am the most fortunate person - to return to Shropshire, to indulge myself in reverie, to allow my mind to lift and to follow gossamer threads of memory, to uncover - to explore again those stored-away days – to rediscover the places, some of the then young faces, some easily and some half-remembered happenings, and to catch with my pen just a little of them, and of me, to their memory and for posterity.

CHAPTER TWO

Arriving at Uckington

If you travel by car along the London to Holyhead Road, attributed at stages of its history to the Romans and to Thomas Telford, when you feel you must be about one more mealtime from the border with Wales, you could be passing through Uckington.

A milestone, low in the hedgerow, used to set the spot to within a few yards. On the short walk to Norton, we read that we were five miles and six furlongs from Shrewsbury, five miles from Wellington, and one hundred and forty-five (that was infinity!) from London. A traveller along the London to Holyhead Road, now stream-coded **A5**, might blink or sneeze, and miss Uckington altogether.

It still appears to consist, as it did in the 1930's, of one large red farmhouse clustered around with its trees and half a dozen cottages a field's depth from one side of the road, and a public house, a garage and, now, a car-park on the other. The car-park is the space where two cottages were, but two more modern dwellings, along the lane to Wroxeter compensate, in number at least, for those missing. Oh, and there used to be a petrol-filling station now, where a five-barred gate used to allow a short-cut passing *The Thatch* to the farmhouse.

I arrived at *The Thatch* with Mum and Dad in early November, 1930, just after my fifth birthday. The correct address was *Number Three, Uckington* and it was one of a pair over the field, opposite the Horse Shoe Inn. Always, though, while we lived there and since, my family have called it *The Thatch*. Perhaps this was because of the impression made on my mother's mind and her personality by the then thatched roof. At least she always held it responsible as host to the fleas which had settled in for the winter and were prepared to defend their territory from such as us. I have to admit to not remembering the actual physical fleas. But I knew that they had been, and of Mum's battle with them because of a permanent stain on the kitchen ceiling - a sort of dark bruise colour. This was the colour of Jeyes Fluid, which had been squirted through a bicycle-pump, soaked through floorboards, fleas and plaster, finally settling into the ceiling whitewash. The stain stood out, a kind of memorial to Mum's persistence. It was still there when we left.

We had the fairly regular farm cottage facilities: two up, two down - and two down the garden. The front door opened directly to the kitchen with its floor of bright red tiles. In the farthest corner was the firegrate. The fire, already lit for us, sprung to extra sparkle as we opened the door. Little orange flames reflected in the black-leaded hob. Above the flames, chain links hung from a metal 'arm', ending with an S-shaped hook for a soot encrusted kettle. Soft whistling came from the side of the grate where part of the hob was a lid to a small boiler. Its gallon or so of water was just beginning to 'sing'. Wisps of smoke trailed back and into the room, whilst Dad and the driver kept opening the door to carry in our furniture.

Beyond, was the back kitchen, with doors to the stairs, to the pantry, and to the wash-house, with its brick built-in washing-boiler, with a fireplace underneath. There was a shallow, brown earthenware sink, with a hole to let out the water, but of course, no taps. A door to the stairhole hid dark-smelling mysteries, like coal, and musty newspaper, and sticks for fire-lighting.

The stairs led directly into the first bedroom. Mine was beyond. I never remember seeing the view from that window, so I simply must have been too small to see through. (We moved to Number Six later.)

But the view from the downstairs at *The Thatch*, especially from the garden I think I must have absorbed it to the extent that my contentment with any future environment was likely to stand or fall by comparison. As other folk may have a pillar, or a particular tree, a distinctive building - or a sign post - or anything whatever which says they are home ... we had a Wrekin! About five miles distant people said it was, but it looked to be at the back of the next field. With changing colour and mood, with time and season, it seemed as lively as a person. Disappointing when hidden in mist, it became teasing and mysterious if only the top was hidden. On clearest days you felt you could almost count its trees, their tops catching the sunlight, and the wind changing their colour - shaded and ruffled like cockerels' feathers.

Mum once said that one of my Grandads had planted some of the trees on the Wrekin. This struck me as strange. I'd always supposed that trees had always been there, right from the beginning - or at very least that they had grown unaided. Fancy anyone planting trees! Even so, I'd been quite certain that something like a Wrekin would have come complete - trees and all - right at the start of all things. Just fancy ... my Grandad ... TREES on the WREKIN!

From the back door, much further westwards, were the Breidens, like two enormous dark blue tents, overlapping on the horizon before the skies of Wales. I always called them, as I still think of them, "The Tent Hills".

Looking away down the back garden path, over fields and woodlands, was Haughmond Hill. Lower, softer, shrubby, almost strokeable, it seemed more like a kitten, compared with the heraldic lion-like Wrekin.

Our "Two down the garden" were reached by a path of solid compressed earth with occasional puddles plugged with broken brick and cinders, to a low brick building with moss-mellowed rooftiles. Through the creaking door an adult could only just stand upright in the tiny whitewashed room, head almost touching the cobwebby rafters. The scrubbed wooden seat was equipped with its neat pile of newspaper squares. The dullest bits of a newspaper could take on a fascination in that dimmest of light, with the somehow reassuring warm feel of the wooden seat. Optimistically the earth closet was called the WC! They explained the "W" stood for ... water?

Most cottages had a pigsty, often sharing a wall with the WC. Ours had a pig in residence for the summers -probably bought with the hay harvest overtime money. He stayed until just before Christmas, when he left to help with the shopping.

The family at the house joined on to us, Number Four, included Joanie (always 'Joanie' - Joan was different and lived at the farm). I always remember Joanie as I first met her, then two years old. She had thick dark hair, bobbed with a fringe, framing a round freckly face with light blue eyes. She wore a light dress - or perhaps it was a jumper - with full-gathered skirt, white socks and dark shoes with button fastenings. With Joanie, as well as her mother and father and, later, a baby brother, lived Grannie and Grandad Beedles and her Aunty Nellie. Perhaps their house was a bit bigger than ours, but it was not at all unusual for three generations, or a family of a dozen or so children to live in "two up - two down" cottages.

From the wicket-gate, looking down the cart-track to the left, was - the Farm House. I could see it, partly hidden amid tall bushes and trees. Large, square and red, its windows were arranged with dignified formality. It had stood through that era when symmetry outside had had to come to terms with fiscal economy. For some of the windows were found, when you got nearer, to be black "pretend" panes with white divisions painted directly onto the bold Shropshire brick.

At the farm lived Joan, a year or two older than me, Barbara, a few days younger, and George, then probably about three. Joan became my very closest friend. Mum said we should call at the farmhouse and invite them to my belated Birthday-Tea.

The farm had two grandmother ladies. Each wore long dark dresses. Real Grannie Evans was round and quiet, perhaps a little bit stern, with a round quiet face. It was Aunty Lizzie who opened the door to us. She was an energetic lady, slimmer and longer in shape, with a narrow pink and white face, and white, wavy hair. There was a shuffling of children's feet in the background, and she shooed them further inside. She explained that the girls were recovering from scarlet fever, so not able to come to our house. She and Mum exchanged a few quiet confidences about infections, and other family matters, and my meeting with Joan and Barbara was delayed.

But Joanie came to tea with us, and for the first of many times brought her 'slickers to put on in the house'.

Chapter Three

Home in the fields

The house which we called *The Thatch* was entirely surrounded by fields. Each had its character, which in time became a part of mine.

Directly continuing from our garden path, through the wicket-gate, was a path worn over the grass, the shortest route to the Main Road, to a wooden five-barred gate opposite the Horse Shoe. A gravel verge, threaded through with camomile and smelling of its crushed feathers and petrol fumes, was a warning, a cautioning to Stop – Look - Listen before going across. Even in those days the London to Holyhead Road was busy. There were a lot of accidents along the half mile or so to Norton.

Vehicles, such as Morriss's bread van, the coal man and, of course, the farm lorry which carried our household effects as well as Mum, Dad and me, had to go 'The Long Way'. Curving to the left inside the big gate a cart-track rounded a small raised 'Planting' of trees, continuing to the right and past our front gate. At *The Planting,* another track, from the road to Norton joined this one. Some distance past *The Thatch,* the hedge on the left came to an end. Here the pit spread into both front and back fields.The pit was home for coots and moorhens. If you stepped very carefully, looking into the dark secret places among the yellow twigs and tangled leaves round the water's rim, you might find a nest. I even had an occasional breakfast of a pinky speckled egg, fried. We understood that the parents would not desert the nest if we did not handle the rest of the eggs. And we would never take more than one at a time. Most winters the pit froze hard enough to slide on.

The track led through another five-barred gate into an enclosure where cows gathered under their short conversational mooing, between field and cowhouse at milking time. And this was where sheep were crowded for mysterious treatment to feet and tails at various seasons. Then they protested with a chorus of baritone bleating. To tread here needed care, through a slush of clay-baked tracks, over, among between - and into - cow-pats and sheep droppings. Here, too, you could be waylaid into watching the colourful antics of myriad insects, like when the sun lit up the amber wings of dung-flies - ('Horse-flies' Mum called them) - a paradox of muck and beauty. We did not worry over-much about messy shoes. Nor, either, did we tolerate them. They were a fact of our lives-the reason for boot-polish. The bright advertisements on Norton Shop did not have to tell us. Shoes got mucky and were cleaned - as we got hungry and were fed. Unwary visitors on town heels were a source of amusement, though not very often.

The next gate, a metal one, had a different feel, a different weight, sang a different tune as it swung and sort of quivered open to let us into the farmyard.

At the far corner of the Front Field, that nearest the Wrekin, iron hurdles replaced the hedges for a stretch, making it safer for people coming out of the lane and into the road. Sometimes a partridge nested in the grass verge, near where the hurdles began. Under the fence and the hedges a bank sloped down to the field. Here among the grass, just as each year was beginning to feel towards spring, came violets. Why is it, I wonder, that even though we know they are there, finding violets is such a surprise? We were surprised last year, too, in exactly the same place. We know they will be there, that is why we look, yet almost unbelieving - and there they are! - smelling of fresh spring rain. After we left Uckington it took me years to find another violet garden.

In wet weather the whole of this corner of the field became boggy, germinant with its own line in wildflowers. It was here I first found the purply-veined lady's smock and the creamy froth of meadowsweet, and what became one of my favourite wildflowers: yellow flag-iris. After long and heavy rain, when the drainage ditch became a stream and the general bogginess a lake, wild ducks swam there, even swans. Mum said all swans belonged to the King.

To the Norton side of the road-gate, still in the Front Field, the level of the field rose higher than the road. A grassy bank, with here and there a dogrose or a bramblebush, sloped down to the short roadside hedge. The top of the bank was a lovely place to be. You could sit and watch the traffic - on Shrewsbury Show days we counted the cars, tried to collect car numbers. Or you could read a book, make daisy-chains, or tussle with sweaty fingers at early knitting. If you felt energetic you could roll down the bank, or you could sit in the sun and dream. And here it was that Alice fell down her rabbit-hole to Wonderland. At least it would have been, had she lived at Uckington. At any rate this is where it would have happened to me, had I been that Alice.

But the real power and purpose behind the reason for the Front Field was marked by a hawthorn bush at the crossing of two footpaths. Even in winter, its bared branches intertwined to a denseness threatening enough to remind anyone who knew to approach with caution. I grew so that I did not approach. The worn path became a doormat-sized bare patch among the grass as it reached a flat stone step - and then another - and then another - going downwards.

Shadowy sandstone lined the hollow. Black, clear and sinister, the water reflected the underside of the bush. From its depth there straggled, as though waving through the still water, green stringy fronds of ... weed? or disintegrating moss ...? or was this what frogspawn looked like ...? or was it really prehistoric ...supernatural ... hair? Belonging to something - somebody - older than the well itself? ! That is what Mum said! At least, she said that was where Ginny Greenteeth lived - and I knew it must be true, because ...there was her hair! I had seen it!

At five or so years old, the world is strange. Strangeness is accepted. That some things were stranger than others, if such matter of degree occurred to a child, was also accepted. Light and dark, winter and summer, burning and freezing. Father Christmas and a thousand other things were inexplicable. When the whole world, it seemed, was magic or incongruous, what was yet another incongruity? Even though this one was that the family's water supply should be housed in the same spot as Ginny Greenteeth, that weird creature whose delight was in stretching her slimy limbs and slithering her stringlike hair, wrapping it tight like green bindertwine round little girls before dragging them under to herself. That this was so I had no doubt, because Dad and Mum had said so - so I had not to go to the Well on my own - not ever! - did I understand ? And that this was so I had no doubt, because if I got anywhere near the place, such was my young imagination that I could all but feel the fingers just shadowing my shoulders, the nearer I got to the well. Being forewarned I never went too close, so I always got away as wet claw-fingers were about to grab me.

She had sisters in other places. Some ponds and streams were decidedly unfriendly (though for some reason not all of them).There was that time when we lived at the other house, at Marton, when Dad and his horses had to drag a poor unwitting cow from the mud. Oh yes. That was the work of one of them. As for those children who fell through the ice and drowned under frozen ponds, well, of course ...

I had nightmares about the water. I still do sometimes. At Uckington I dreamt I saw a pond, high up on a grassy bank, Alice's bank. From the pond's edges dozens of pairs of children's shoes and boots were running. Each had miniature legs and feet grown from its sole. Their owners having received the Ginny Greenteeth treatment, these hapless shoes were being carried by strange little running legs down the grassy slope towards the busy Main Road! Perhaps I had been hearing about the Pied Piper - I don't know. Oh, her associates were legion, but she, the arch-spirit of sinister water, dwelt in the well under the hawthorn bush in our Front Field.

Later, we no longer fetched water from the well. Concern for Public Health because of a diphtheria epidemic led to a change of source. Thence we carried our buckets along to the farmyard, to a tap which topped a hygienic grey pipe, and we staggered them home along the cart-track.

> *There is one thing I wonder:*
> *Will someone ever tell*
> *What became of Ginny Greenteeth*
> *When they drained away her well?*

If the fields to the side and the back of *The Thatch* lacked the charisma of the Front Field, they nevertheless had their own significant influence on my early years. The one at the side always comes to mind with songs about the countryside with corn and long grass, like:

"*Amid the acres of the rye ...*

Those pretty country folk would lie ..." and:

"*Comin' through the rye..*", and so on.

Not that we knew rye as a crop then. It was something we heard about in songs, like nightingales.

But our Side Field seemed to have a steady rotation of other grain crops, as well as grass and clover. As grain and clover grew towards summer and waved with rustling whispers, they lent themselves to a forming and sharing of secrets, and this was a place to retreat with private thoughts. I remember it, too, when I think about harvest, or long grass – that is where the picture takes me, to the Side Field, smelling and sounding of summer and me in the sun, sitting and thinking.

Gardens as I remember them were for growing food – basic vegetables and fruit, flowers, and chickens. It was generally a poor gardener who left uncultivated patches for children to philosophise in. Lawns did not feature in many cottagers' gardens. They came later, with 'better' times, and a spreading of 'bourgeois' inclinations. So to sit and think, we found a spot in a field, usually under the hedgerow. We knew better than to flatten the growing corn.

If you followed a track near the hedge, not the hedge near the road, you could eventually reach the Bottom Field – a short-cut to Mrs Stephenson's shop at Norton. You still had to cross at the cross roads, but mothers preferred that to the busy road way, where there was no curb, just an irregular grass verge - but more about such journeying later.

An iron hurdle at the end of the back garden-path, between the pigsty and the chicken-run, was a stile to climb over to the Back Field, with its own character. The grass, coarser than the front, sloped tuftily away from the house. You needed to keep to the tracks of flattened grass. To stray could land you in a strange smelling soggy area, where the 'sock' drained from our domestic arrangements. It was not altogether foul smelling, just – well, strange and stale and distinctive. Mothers did not like it on shoes and socks.

The Back Field was not encouraged for playing. Neither was it quite forbidden, for it was a helpful short-cut to the stackyard, especially if cows barred the usual way. I suppose I was allowed through the Back Field, more or less on trust. And that trust, I confess, I broke more often than was known. For just behind the pigsty blocks, immediately in the field, conveniently out of sight of the house, was *The Forbidden Place*.

To venture into the heart of the rubbish-tip was a journey to be undertaken with eyes alert and breath held. Carefully treading, you tested your weight, with sturdy sandals between jutting daggers of broken earthenware and slippery round bottles. To judge it wrongly would be to be found out. Ragged edges of rusty cans waited to trap and inform. A cut or a scratch from rusty things turned to blood-poisoning – Mum said. I couldn't picture the detailed reality of blood-poisoning, but it sounded nasty, and not the kind of thing you could hide. So one false move, and they could know where I had been.

The tip was a world of treasure – such fuel for the firing of imagination. For as well as the odd broken cup, milk-jug, leaking saucepan, empty Germoline tin recently thrown there, were all the intriguing discards – bottles, tins, china, kitchen things – it seemed, of all the families who had ever lived at *The Thatch*. Tantalising fragments of plain or heavily ornamented china, with curved edges, flat rims, fluted shell-like hollow shapes were all displayed and yet hidden in a random jumble. Sometimes there was enough to tell what the piece had been a part of – often not. Often you were left to conjecture their original shape, what they were used for ... and by whom? What was last cooked in that cracked old pan? What else did they eat? What were their names? Who drank from the rosebud cup – and who broke it? – or the plate with the blue-gold rim? How did it look when it was clean? Exploring, persistent fingers with spit and a dock-leaf did their best to find out ... They would have been ordinary belongings of ordinary people in their ordinary lives, most likely, but to a mind searching for adventure, they could have served a king – or entertained angels.

It would have been lovely to have found just one item complete, but people did not throw away whole things. Sometimes enamel dishes, bowls or mugs, white showing through the sooty grime, looked whole until you rubbed them clean, but they always had holes. The object I would most have liked to find whole was a candle-stick, one of those white enamel ones with a coloured rim, flattish shape, a sort of built-in plate for a matchbox, and a flat ribbon-like handle in a bow at the side. The shape always delighted me, and we didn't use candles, but little lamps for bedtime. There was something kind of basic, well-balanced – earthily-original – about the shape of a candlestick. It gave a feeling of dependability – of a kind of timelessness – satisfying. I found the feeling, too, in shapes like milking-stools, and the sort of symmetry in pictures of Miss Muffet's spider. I once thought I had found a good candle-stick, but when I disentangled it from the springy nettle-stalks, its handle slumped from the joint where the enamel had flaked away. Yes, it would have been nice to have found something complete, but there was reward in the searching. That, and the guilt of being in *The Forbidden Place*, were compensation for each other.

CHAPTER FOUR

Roots in the farmyard

"Rural children are intellectually inferior to their urban contemporaries."

Now you probably don't believe that. I certainly don't. It was some decades after my Uckington years that I read those words of an eminent Child Psychologist. His argument was that lack of urban social stimulus leads inevitably to dull country children. Since then I have wondered how much time he had spent with children on a farm. All my life I have felt that children who did not enjoy my own childhood's rich rural background were the ones deprived.

I have tried to imagine what could have replaced freedom to grow and to explore at will among the seasons and the life of the countryside; what sort of urban activity replace the chance to mingle with, and share the lives of, farm animals - even experimentally nibbling with them at the crops. We would not have cared for a whole meal of raw mangold, but to select and sample from the piles in the stackyard, to taste the crisp earth freshness through gappy teeth, was only one of such options which we took for granted. The same with sugarbeet found lying at the side of the road to school, the sweet whiteness was more familiar to us than whole coconut, though not dissimilar in texture. I can still feel the pinky flecks of bran running through my fingers, and the smell of it in the granary where so many other things were. I have felt my body could have grown strong, and satisfied, on the smell alone.

Wet Saturday afternoons were spent in the granary, making 'houses' among the sacks, nibbling a mixture of bran and maizeflakes, and the bon-bons coated with powdery sugar which Mum bought for us in Shrewsbury on Saturday mornings.

And in the fields, too ... When they told us about when Jesus plucked the ears of corn - even on the Sabbath - we understood. We knew why He did it. For we, too knew the taste of the milky kernel - and the feel of smooth silky grains on our fingertips - with the smell of green-growing (and of gold-ripening) all around us. Once we watched part of the building of a Dutch barn. It seemed as though the tall iron posts would tiptouch the sky before silvery corrugated segments were joined then curved together piece by piece, constraining it into a gigantic roof, and to earthly bounds. They said it was a Dutch barn. Plainly it was built by someone named Smith from Whitchurch. It said so on a blue and white enamel label.

There were other such barns in the stackyard. Full of straw they gave us shelter from the wind. But when they were not yet full, or later half used to a modest height we could climb a stack from convenient footholes, to a ledge, wide enough for a good sized floor. Up here we could build dens, or even 'houses' with sheaves or bales.

We sat among the creamy gold straw, among all the smells of harvest, and played talking games. We played at 'favourites', named favourite flowers, favourite colours, Christian names and changed our own accordingly. We named favourite filmstars, though we knew most of them only from their faces on cigarette cards begged from our elders, or scavenged from empty packets at the roadside.

We talked of who we wished we were, where we'd like to be, what we would do when we grew up. And we wove fantasy around our relatives, worked hard to impress about the doings of parents, grandparents, or others real or imaginary. Usually we did not convince each other. But sometimes we did and that brought problems.

Some days, after being taken seriously, I was

questioned by Dad:

"What's this about your Aunty Ede getting married? - and HOW many bridesmaids ..."

Or- "What have you been saying about Uncle Harry? Going abroad? to WHERE??"

"And when did Granma have...WHAT disease was it?"

"You wanta watch what you'm sayin' another time! You munna tell tales like that!"

I didn't think I could tell tales so convincingly. Trouble was, I did not have one of those limitless families. I had six aunties and uncles, mostly unmarried, but the farm family knew them all, and I could not get away with much invention. And the scope and the atmosphere of our world high up in the gathered corn, did so lend itself to more than ordinary happenings to the ordinary beings who peopled our families, and therefore our world.

I would like to take you with me round some of the farmyard as I remember it. To help with a word-picture, I need to ask you please to try to imagine a large capital letter 'E'. That is a much simplified pattern of the main farm buildings. Then, if you would place an equally large capital 'I' opposite the open side of the 'E', with a narrow space between them, the 'I' will roughly represent the farmhouse, continuing to a row of buildings which included pig sties, carthouses and the granary above. The space in between the 'E' and the 'I' is the farmyard. And the stackyard is right at the back of the 'E'.

Now the top bar of the 'E' and about a third of the back, formed the milking cowhouses, with stalls and mangers where the cows were tethered. The middle bar of the 'E' was wider, roughly square, entered by a door opposite to the farmhouse, with a way right through to the stackyard. Either side of the way through, cattle were herded loosely, when conditions required it. Though almost dark compared with outdoors, it felt peaceful, and comfortably smelly, and the animals seemed content.

They had hay and linseed cattle-cake to chew, and pinky brown rocksalt lollipops almost the size of milestones, to lick with their floppy wet tongues.

The bottom bar of the '*E*' shape, the end nearest *The Thatch*, formed the stable block. There was an exception to our freedom to play in the farm-buildings as fancy moved us. The stables were quiet, serious, respectable. If the farmyard had held an aspidistra, I feel it would have lived in the parlour-like stable. Perhaps it was that the waggoners were less tolerant of children at play, or that as we well knew - horses were especially sensitive. For whatever reason, when we entered the stable, it was respectfully, by invitation, into a solemn atmosphere. The rafters, higher than light from the small windows could penetrate, were hidden up among the shadows. Stalls of wood the thickness of brick walls, with solid mangers, looked as though they could have grown there and the stable been built around them. Half of the stalls were home to Dad's horses, the others to Mr. Luther's. (He was Dot's Grandfather.)

Heavy wooden coffers stood, one under each window, one for each waggoner. Lids shone, brushed by the sleeves of cotton denim slops over year, after year, after year. Some of the atmosphere was perhaps due to the solemn ritual of grooming and feeding and harnessing and cleaning and polishing. In the gloom you could feel the gleam on the tackle and the sheen on the horses. Such light as found its way into the stable, picked out the buckles and other brass bits where they shone with caring. The powerful smell of the dubbin and of the horses was quite different from anywhere else on the farm.

The bond between waggoners and carthorses was something to stay deep, deep in memory. Almost mystical, the sensitive partnership was born of caring, and strength, and of skilful responsiveness – all these and a wisdom learned about the work to be done in the fields.

Every single day, except Sundays, horses and men were together from sometimes before earliest dawn to later than sunset. Dad went with a hurricane-lamp to groom and breakfast them before his own breakfast, and fed and tended them before his own rest. And sometimes, as he slept, the night rang with his calls to them as in dreams he rounded the fields with them yet again.

The rest of the main 'backbone' of the 'E' picture was made up of smaller rooms and looseboxes. One was the Chaff Room, where we plunged our hands into the crumbly feel of a pyramid of silky gold husks from threshed corn. For all I then knew the famous Pyramids consisted of crumbly chaff. Over all of these rooms was a loft, smelling of clean hessian sacks and like the inside of a flour-bag - and to which I have returned in my dreams many times over the years.

Along the whole of the long wall with doorways leading in from the stackyard, was a gangway. It gave access to the looseboxes and various other places, and to the mangers where the cows were tethered for milking. Two iron rails ran the length of it, and a heavy wooden truck carried food and stuff to the occupants.

When cows were in for milking, we could walk quietly and meet them face to face over the mangers, between the wooden bars at the front of their stalls. Again I have asked myself - suppose we had been town children, deemed by that psychologist gentleman to have been 'more intelligent' because of our 'superior environment', what might have taken the place of seeing my own reflection in those pools of brown velvet which were cows' eyes? - and of smelling the sweet crunched hay on their breath as they chewed the cud, seemingly to eternity? And which urban sounds would have been preferable to the sharp striking of milk into empty metal buckets, tone changing and deepening as the swishes became liquid thuds, rhythmically punching the steamy milk from udder to bucket - after bucket - after bucket?

When the cows had left for the fields, the stalls sluiced down, the sun and the wind drying the cowhouse floors, the same area was a different game altogether. For the six or so of us had the time of our lives.

We gave each other rides in the gangway truck. Taking it in turns, most of us could ride. One or two could easily push the rest. Once started along the shiny rails, the wheels and the loaded coach gained speed surprisingly quickly. A slight bend about halfway along, near the double doors, made it all the more realistic.

Excitement overflowed as we diddly-di-bumped with screams and squeals round the last half corner to the final stretch. If we didn't brake soon enough, there was the thrill of crashing into the bumpers at the end. We ran and we rode and we squealed and we laughed till we ached with the stitch and couldn't speak for tears of fun!

Looking back, I sometimes wonder that we enjoyed such tremendous freedom, at the core of what I now understand to be a serious, scientific and as we might now say capital-intensive business. But freedom we had. And I feel it must have been through a measure of mutual respect and of trust. Because we saw and understood so much about the crops and animals, we shared some of the responsibility; not by working, as the adults did, but I believe through our attitude. Behaviour in that respect must have been almost intuitive. We would no more have misused that fun with the truck track than the adults would have. We would not have upset the cows' need of peace. We knew when to keep a quiet distance, well - most of the time.

Not that we were always virtuous. We could be naughty. One black moment which went deep was when we were walking up the back lane with Joan's Grandad Evans. He was really cross. I can hear his stern voice –

"If anything like this happens again, I shall BAN Selina from the premises!"

(Nobody then, even grown-ups, except at school, called me 'Selina', except when it was really serious.) It could have been a death- sentence. I cannot remember what the misdemeanour was, but I remember going home, very subdued, and asking Mum what 'premises' meant.

One night a different disaster struck. Children and adults were shattered. We had moved to Number Six by then, and the first evidence of trouble was solemn faces, subdued voices and unusual activity when I called early one morning at the farmhouse. We talked about it all the way to school, at school and all the way home. When we'd said all there was to say over and over again, we could still think of nothing else. What had happened was this. The building which was mostly the cowhouse included some smaller rooms, one of which was home for the bull. Over the whole was a loft used to store sacks of potatoes, among other things. During the night of disaster, the loft gave way and the load of hundredweight sacks had collapsed on top of the bull - and squashed him. I think it was Joanie's Dad who found him. Mr Beedles was the stock-man. We were stunned. And when the numbness thawed, we wept. We could not sleep for thinking of the horror of it. The memory of the feel of it still makes me go gooseflesh.

Right on the corner of the cowhouse building was a room distinguished from outside by a chimney. It was called the Saddle Room, though it was far from the stables. Right in its corner farthest from the door, was a little fireplace, with a mantelpiece, an awning of black iron for the draught, and a tiny hob with a trivet, and a fender. The room was furnished with a couple of oldish chairs, a table and even a bed, and there was coconut matting on the floor. The Saddle-Room was important to us children for two reasons. At busiest times of the year, harvesting or sugarbeet-hoeing times, two interesting characters came to join the farmworkers. Sam's face was round, cheerful and sunset-coloured. His brother Ned's was rather longer, more serious, with a lighter shade of tan. Both wore red and white neckerchiefs. We children were always glad to see them. Grownups warned us not to make a nuisance of ourselves - or to keep the men from their work - but we did love to hear their stories. They brought adventure to us with their lively company. During stays at the farm, Sam and Ned lived in the Saddle Room. No one seemed to know where they were when they were not at Uckington - or to be surprised when they came - or when they went. They appeared at the farm – and went - as the seasons did.

Our consolation at their leaving came in that we could then play in the Saddle-Room. Our 'houses' in the stackyard and the granary were fine, but at best only 'pretend'. In the Saddle-Room we had real furniture - and a real fireplace. We even cooked a sort of meal - intended to be stew. Being rich in ideas but poor in practice, it was beyond our skill to keep a fire in long enough to cook carrots and onions and potatoes. It was then I learnt how long carrots can take to cook through. None of us really had the heart to admit that we didn't actually like eating warm, hard vegetables, even flavoured with an Oxo cube, as well as with woodsmoke. I don't think we knew about salt then, but we tried, and enjoyed the trying.

And we could plan things from the Saddle-Room. The Flag Day, for instance. Like all children we were continually short of money. We worked hard all one Saturday, with smoke stew for dinner, drawing Union Jacks and colouring them with wax crayons. We had been learning about the crosses of the patron saints, so the flags were authentic. But there was not a lot of scope among ten houses for door to door sales, and we were disappointed that even they did not take us seriously. We wondered why everyone was so certain that our collection was not 'official'. Our own mothers found us a few consolation coppers, but Mum said that was not how real flag days were organised. No one could tell us, though, what we should have done to make it 'real'.

Our small proceeds went the way of most of our spending-money, through the back door at the Horse Shoe, to Mrs Walton, on crisps and chocolate wafers.

I have to resist an inclination to describe the 1930s Uckington farmhouse garden inch by inch and plant by plant. Yet I must recount something of its atmosphere, paying it tribute as host to so many hours and years of imaginings. It says something of our friendship and of our sharing of experiences of growing and exploring, that much of the farm children's home and particularly their garden, is as deeply set in my mind as the one with Mum and Dad at home. Like the periwinkle-place, the snowball bushes, the laurels that smelt of almonds when we crushed their leaves, like the mud-pie pantry under the evergreens near the orchard, the two-hole WC with 'Woman and Home' and their free-gift dress patterns for lavatory paper, the climbing-place from the orchard where we could get to hide on a roof behind the granary, the clump of holly and yew trees by the small yard gate opposite the stables; the place between the snowball bushes and the back of the farmhouse, where once I came face to face, so to speak, with a hung sheep in the process of being butchered - and my confused impression of familiar wool and creamy underside and stuff I thought better than to stop to identify. I ran and ran, but could not get away from the horror of the picture.

There was the big lawn with the daffodils patch in the corner where the grass grew long, and the see-saw and the cade lambs' tether, and the swing in the great tree which looked over all. There was the tiny lawn by the French- window, where once we sat and rehearsed a song:-

"*Will you come to Abyssinia will you come?*
Bring your own bread and butter and your bun."

or was it, '*ammunition and your gun*'? - perhaps it had two

versions -
> *"Mussolini will be there, shooting bullets in the air!*
> *Will you come to Abyssinia will you come?"*

They borrowed the tune for that from a very different song:

> *"Roll along covered-wagon roll along,*
> *To the turns of your wheels I'll sing a song:*
> *City ladies may be fine, but give me that girl of mine,*
> *Roll along covered-wagon, roll along."*

The original 'Country and Western', perhaps? Perhaps not. For some reason there was a kind of romantic interest in caravans, covered-wagons, the gypsy life. A favourite and typical song with a feel of the times was:

> *"Oh, play to me, gypsy,*
> *The moon's high above,*
> *Oh, play me a serenade,*
> *A song I love.*
> *Beside your caravan, your camp fire's* bright,
> *I'll be a vagabond, just for tonight.*
> *Oh, play to me gypsy,*
> *And when you are gone*
> *Your song will be haunting me*
> *And lingering on."*

Lingering on - that was right.

Nearly everybody's favourite poem at school was 'The Pedlar's Caravan' -

> *"I wish I lived in a caravan,*
> *With a horse to drive like a pedlar-man*
> *Where he comes from nobody knows,*
> *Nor where he goes to, but on he goes."*

- and on he went for several verses, I can only remember snatches.

But back to the garden: sometimes on the tiny lawn we did useful jobs, shelling peas, slicing beans, polishing knives and forks. We were rewarded at least once with new potatoes and kidney beans, almost floating in butter. We filled baskets and basins with raspberries and gooseberries for the farmhouse kitchen. It was accepted that we ate a few - and even stuffed a few goosegogs under our knicker elastic to eat later.

The walled and cobbled houseyard is memorable on three counts. Here the dairy, nearly all windows, with gleaming silvery churns and buckets and measuring things was joined on to the farmhouse back kitchen. Then the high house wall was free from windows, perfect for ball-against-the-wall games. Three of us could play at once.

And the third thing: housed in a wooden purpose built shed was something more ferocious than all the animals. It shattered the peace of the farmyard and its surroundings early every morning and late every afternoon. Anyone quietly dreaming would start with terror at the sudden outburst: BBRRRRRR ... TTTTTTT ... THUMP THUMP THUMP THUMP ...

I suppose that earlier inventions had in their own way affected life on the farm: the binder which tied up sheaves as it cut the corn, the threshing-machine, telephone. The tractor had a class of its own at the Ploughing Match by now. But the arrival of the milking-machine must have been most revolutionary in its effect on the atmosphere of the farmyard itself. Everyone knew it was there. At the cows' end, fortunately it was relatively quiet, no more than gentle hissing and a chinkling of the connections as the men moved from one to another, attaching the cows by their teats to an arrangement of, well sort of hosepipes and glass buckets. It struck me as being a bit like my French knitting with stitches over nails into cotton-reels.

But as for the generator, after its first unmusical outburst, it settled to a rhythmic throb which resounded throughout the whole procedure. It drowned conversation in its immediate vicinity, and beyond that told the whole neighbourhood when milking started – and when it finished. All sorts of speculations were considered when it began earlier or later than usual.

Of the buildings beyond the houseyard, the most interesting to us was probably the pigsties - a whole row of them. Often one was pig free - and of course, clean. That came in for yet another pretend-house, or a shop for Joan and Barbara, or a place to store and change into dressing-up clothes. Once we secretly peeped through a slit in the dividing wall into the next sty - and watched the birth of a baby pig. We didn't suppose we ought to stay for more than one.

About halfway along the carthouses was the garage, where lived the big Wolseley motor car, plum-red, with a black top. We valued the dimension of adventure that added to our otherwise sheltered lives.

At the very far end of all the buildings was a single door, to the stairs up to the granary. From upstairs in the granary a loading door overlooked the lane and the gardens and the cottages at Numbers Five, Six and Seven. Opposite the first granary door, over the wide expanse of the yard, was the loading ramp, where the animals went in, two by two, or whatever number, to the lorries which took them to market.

Round the corner past the ramp a gateway led to the stackyard, another to the backfield, and a third into a small '*Patch*' field, where the large chicken house stood, and where we were set to search round the foot of the hedges for eggs laid into 'stolen' nests. It was in *The Patch* that in due season we found mushrooms. The ladies at the farmhouse made them into ketchup, and we talked about how the maggots wriggled out of the mushrooms. It was in this field, too, that we once laughed ourselves into hysterics, playing 'tick' around the henhouse, with a growing up cade lamb at about the same stage of playful development as ourselves.

That was where the lane came up from Upton Magna. The station was, I suppose, half an hour or so's walk. The lane came past Numbers Eight and Nine

Uckington where Pughs and Wainwrights lived. It curved round Number Five's garden, noted the farmyard opposite, continued under the granary's loading door, past the small stockyard with a rickety barn, past the white front gate of the farmhouse. Then, it wound for another five minutes or so, to the main road, and the hurdles near the violet place, and the partridge nest, where I took you once before.

Chapter Five

To Donnington after Whit

It was as though all the June days of Earth's Golden Ages were epitomised in the brilliance which was that First of June. The sun shone early - and so did we.

"You won't need a coat. Just take your cardigan," Mum said. "Be careful not to lose it. Keep it in your schoolbag when you're not wearing it. Don't lose your handkerchief either. Always put that back in your pocket."

Dot, Barbara and Joan were coming along the field path as we reached the wicket. They could have taken me, but Mum was coming too – "Being as it's the first day," she said.

There had been a difference of opinion as to when I should start school. I had been five since the end of October, but Mum had her own view about the right time for my legs to start walking the two and a half miles or so along the lanes and over the fields from Uckington to Donnington. A few weeks earlier Dot had knocked with a message.

"Please, Mrs Farlow, the Master says he is starting a new register after Easter and would you send Selina to school then?"

A what? And whatever had whatever it was to do with my being at school?

"Oh, no," Mum answered firmly, "I have told him all along she will start after Whit, not before. Tell him she will come then."

Now at last our shadows walked beside us over the field as the remains of a summer mist lifted from the Wrekin. That was the day my shadow changed shape because of the schoolbag. Each day for many years the bag was to hold meatpaste 'pieces' in a paper-bag, and a medicine-bottle filled with lemonade. I could feel the liquid slurp as I walked. We'd bought the lemonade crystals specially from Woolworths on Saturday.

The quarter to eight Sentinel hooter found us about to cross the busy main road, the creamy soles of my new sandals getting green and sticky with the grass and the flowers.

"All get together to cross! And look both ways!"

Dot was the big girl. Over we went, across the yard of the garage, over the end of the lane to Wroxeter and into Beslow lane, between the Horse Shoe's wall and Mrs Habberley's house.

"You'm in good time today!" a voice called through waving arms and a white table-cloth. Mrs Habberley was a Granma lady. I believe she told the time of year as well as of the day by our passing. She seemed to watch out for us. I expect she missed us in the holidays.

We passed the pond where later I tried to skim the surface with a flat stone and where, on another day, I fell over a pothole and collected a scar on my knee to last my lifetime.

The lane and the journey had many diversions. No wonder we needed plenty of time. Over the years we were to measure the seasons by its hedgerows, its birdsnests and birdsong, by its quickening twigs - and by the jewelled webs of its autumns. We tasted seasonal treats from its sorrel, its blackberries and sweetbriar – and its shed sugarbeet.

On this June day we stepped through the lane's gleam and its shade, its sunshafts and its shadows. Blackbirds and thrushes sang from the branches and fluttered to secret places among the May blossom. From the bridge over the Bell Brook, we could watch our faces mirrored, and framed in watercress. Up the bank and past the dogrose hedge with the yellow hammer's place, the lane turned sharply by Podmores' and Jebbs' houses. (Teeces moved to Podmores' later.)

Mrs Jebb kept a sort of shop in her house, where

we could buy sweet cigarettes and chewy coconut pretend tobacco, liquorice bootlaces and yellow packets of cali with liquorice straws through which to suck and then splutter the fizzy powder. Jelly babies, dolly mixtures, aniseed-balls, gobstoppers, pear-drops and chocolate bars, her house was an Aladdin's cave of penny and ha'penny treasures. Almost always Mrs Jebb wore a blue dress, her dark hair parted in the middle. She had a daughter, Monica, who was a nurse and had hair the colour of new pennies, plaited and coiled into 'earphones'.

A stile in the corner by Podmores' house led to a short-cut, or otherwise we walked through the farmyard.

Beslow's farmers were the Crow family. We thought the young Mr Crow looked like the Prince of Wales. Towards the end of our Donnington days, he got married. We were very excited about this because his wife was so beautiful. She was elegant and gracious and wore such wonderful clothes. 'The Gorgeous Mrs Crow' we called her. She outshone all the film stars on our cigarette cards. What is more, SHE walked and she waved, SHE smiled and she spoke to US. She even seemed to like US. We vied with each other for a glimpse of her. Sometimes the Master gave us notes to deliver to Beslow farm, then we were quite beside ourselves. Ah, the Gorgeous Mrs Crow! Can she ever have known what joy she brought to our lives?

Our way through their farmyard and the fields beyond included several five-barred gates, easing our way through herds of young bullocks. They were quite passive: they never tried to argue when we fastened the gate firmly behind us.

It was from the tracks of these last two fields that I was most aware of being surrounded by mountains. Not close, to crowd us or to make our world smaller, they were far away, beyond all the fields. Like a frame round a picture, they seemed to hold our world together - and at the same time tell us that all of the rest of creation and everything which was 'foreign' lay somewhere beyond them. Except for the Wrekin and nearby Charlton and Haughmond Hills - we were not certain which were which, or where one range ended and another began, for they merged and overlapped on our horizon.

They signalled the progress of our years with changing light and colour. Snow came to them earlier than it did to us, and it stayed longer. Sometimes when we were in shade, we could watch patches of sunlight moving among the mounds and the folds of them. When there was a rainbow, it might have been growing from one of their craggy sides. We took them for granted, as we did the grass and the hedges. When eventually I left Shropshire it was the feeling of my world being held in place by the hills that I missed most of all. For all that I learnt in geography lessons I seemed not to have understood that all people did not share a similar horizon. Stupid of me, but there it was - part of the shock of my uprooting.

From half a field away, we could see the roof of the school and the high back wall of the open shed. We could see the Master's house among the trees. From here too we could look left to the neighbouring field, and see tiny figures which gradually enlarged into the Pritchards and the Joneses and the Coggins and the Lowes and the Rawlings and the Foulkeses and the rest of the Uppington and Wheathill Ones. Our paths would not meet for another half mile or more.

We had yet to pass the pond where we could spend dinner-times sliding when the frost was hard enough (once someone fell in, but it was not seriously deep) - and the spot where one day we were to watch preparations for the electricity pylon, the ground being gouged away by the Giro-Tiller.

Through another gate, into another lane by the Williams' house, and we were under the walnut trees. Every autumn we foraged for fallen nuts, burning lips and fingers in our impatience. The fleshy green covering resisted as we hacked it away in silly pieces. Its sap stained us to a purply tan. After the second, hard shell was cracked we could still have used something like a Giro-Tiller action to scoop out the curly kernel. Even then, teeth had to peel away the bitter yellow skin. How much more sensible to have waited until they were ripe, and yet how urgent our conquest seemed.

At the other side of the lane, what we called 'gilly'-flowers grew from a wall which continued round the Master's garden and the school playground. Rounding its point at the end of the lane, we could meet a whole crowd: the Rogers boys and the Leake girls, the Hardings, the Butlers, the Browns and the Carters, the Parrys, the Shores and all the other Wroxeter and the Norton Ones, and the Starlings, Teeces and other Ones who lived nearer. The Blounts and the Lewises and the rest of the Charlton Hill Ones, along with the Uppington Ones, met us at the school gate. By nine o'clock, all sixty or so of us had passed over the dusty playground. Probably less than six lived in Donnington itself, and fewer than another six had less than one mile to walk. The reason for the school being where it was is another story altogether. (It is sometimes called Donnington under the hill to distinguish it from Shropshire's better known Donnington.)

The school was as near to our homes as it was to a bus-route. On days of absolutely torrential rain farmers would fit a journey to school around the milking, but daily journeys by car were unthinkable. Always, it was walk and run, explore and dream, think and talk - and sometimes fall out - all the way and every day.

On that June day, Mum walked with me the whole length of the Big School Room, from the Girls' Porch Door to the Master's desk at the far end. I saw the Master as a square sort of man, with a squarish head and shoulders, his mouth in a straight line on his squarish face, with smooth hands with hard knuckles and stubby fingertips.

As we stood at his desk, Mum insisted to him that I was born in 1925. He insisted that, as this was 1931 and I was five – "She MUST have been born in 1926. You've got it wrong." He appeared to go on believing this for the next several years, despite my October birthday.

Meanwhile his wife took charge of me. I remember the Mistress as a lady without angles. It was as though every part of her was smoothed outwards softly. Her hands and fingers shone as though covered - stretched over - with pale, translucent satin. The colour and the smoothness might have flowed over either from, or to, her opal ring.

Her forehead, face and neck followed their own continuous line. Grey-gold hair lay in smooth waves close to the roundness of her head, then into a bun at the back. Under the bun was the jewelled clasp of her pearl necklace. Her shoulders, arms and the rest of her might have been poured for moulding into dark silk dresses.

She was a strict, no-nonsense teacher. Formality was the breath of her.

On this first day, her stern eyes took me apart through round spectacles in narrow gold frames. She opened the half-glass door to the Infants Room and, with her other hand, propelled me to my first entrance. A hubbub of undersound hushed, and about twenty faces, arranged in pairs, took me in.

One or two faces I thought I knew, but when the Mistress asked, "Who knows Selina?", it was a stranger's hand which shot up in an instant.

"Very well," responded the Mistress, and to me she said, "Go and sit next to that girl. She will look after you."

The face under the arm of the shot-propelled hand flushed and stared at me as I sat at the other half of the double desk. This was not one of my friends from Uckington. I had never seen this girl before. Why had she said she knew me?

Soon I understood. To get promotion you had to

push a bit. This was one of those times when cut and thrust had to take the place of accuracy. My 'truth' illusion shattered, this girl dealt with another.

"You must be quiet in school," Mum had said. "Don't speak to the other children except at playtime."

The Mistress was sitting at her desk, a large book open in front of her. So that was the Register. From it she read everyone's name. Each child answered in turn – "Yessum." I found that "Um" had to be added whenever we spoke to the Mistress. She never explained why.

She closed the Register, moved her chair and turned to the blackboard. In this, the slightest of rustling, the girl beside me leaned my way. With her hand before her mouth and her eyes still looking to the front of her, she twisted her lips in my direction and hissed. At another calculated moment she hissed again. As she tried yet again, the hissing was beginning to shape itself into recognisable words: "Can you do SUMS?" I was clearly trying the patience of this cut and thrust person. But I was not practised at whispering, so I went on pretending not to understand.

The worst part of being a new infant at Donnington School was that first thing every afternoon we were required to rest, supposedly to sleep. The idea was reasonable enough, considering the length of our day, and the long walk most of us had each way.

In practice, the 'rest' involved spreading a dark grey blanket over a strip of floor between the last row of desks and the gloss-painted brown wall. The blanket smelt of chalk and carbolic and of plasticine, and the floor smelt of dusty boards and of such of the outdoors as may cling to children's shoes. We were to lie on our stomachs, dinner-time paste pieces, jam butties and all, heads on our hands - and go to sleep whilst the older ones went on with their lessons.

I have never been less comfortable. Those hours were the longest and the hardest of all my years at school.

For draughts played on my bare knees and my twisted neck. Pins and needles found my pillow-hands and sleep kept well away.

"A time and a place for everything," was one of Mum's sayings, and this time and this place were not for sleep and me together. For the most part I enjoyed school. For all my late beginning, I took to reading and writing. Arithmetic held a kind of logic which my mind was able to follow - at least most of the time. And I was blessed with a mind which, in those days at least, was able to learn and remember.

Once I was past the age for having to sleep on the floor, my memories of the *Infants Room* were happy. Best of all were Monday, Wednesday and Friday afternoons. That was when the boys from the Infants joined the other boys in the Big Room - and all the girls came into the *Infants Room* for Sewing.

Chapter Six

Sewing days at Donnington

Our earliest stitches were large and brightly coloured. With blunt-ended needles and thick thread, we created all varieties of crosses, diamonds, triangles on to a crash fabric with even-spaced holes. Soon we progressed to a finer smooth linen, still with bold cotton stitches. Now we were exhorted to "Be sure to count your threads! Woe betide the girl who gets her stitches uneven!" "Woe betide ...!" began many of the Mistress's warnings.

Soon we were practising basic sewing seams. It did not dare cross anyone's mind that such seams might have been done by machine. Our task was to learn the craft of sewing. Machining was something for the future.

"Run and Fell is the seam we use when the work has to lie flat," the Mistress explained. "French seams enclose the edges to lie on the inside of your work."

As we threaded needles from the big tacking reel, we were prodded by her voice:

"Betty! Which stitches do we use for tacking?"

"A long stitch and then a short one, um."

"Quite right. Everybody! Which stitches for a running seam?"

"Three runs and a back stitch, um," we chorused.

"And HOW do we fasten off?"

"Three stitches on the same spot, um." Again we chanted.

There were no short-cuts. Presspleating, pinning, tacking, sewing, opening out and trimming, the whole procedure repeated to completely enclose the raw edge, in all it was a matter of working each seam's length as many as ten times. By then, white calico had taken up blood from punctured fingers.

"In which direction do we oversew?"

"From the left side to the right side, um."

"And which direction for hemming?"

"From the right side to the left side, um."

It was not only a matter of working on practice pieces. Seams and hems added up to pillowcases, aprons and other things.

"Tell your mothers you are going to make pillow slips in good quality *Horrocks'* cotton calico. They will cost sixpence each if your mother wishes to buy one."

I never see or hear the name *Horrocks* without hearing her voice. Something of her own forthrightness burst forth on the sound. Folding and cutting the calico was an experience. So crisp, it crackled and it sparkled flashing white as she measured and folded. She snipped into the selvedge and the tearing sound as she dragged the pieces apart lives on for me in sliding trombones.

"When seams and hems are completed, you will learn to sew on the tapes for fastenings."

We made simple dresses. They needed facings cut out on the cross, and even our own-made bias binding. The theory and the plan for the strips were worked out and thoroughly understood on paper first.

We learned to do different types of pleating - and to gather into a band. I can still feel the pressure of the needle against fabric against my finger as we pushed ... and stroked - pushed ... and stroked ... along the tight rows of drawn up gathering thread. When all lay neatly in line, the thread was loosened to fit the band.

Buttonholes were plotted on paper, stitch by pencil stitch, along a line which represented the cut.

"Buttonhole stitches on the straight and over-stitches at the corners. How many stitches at each corner?"

"Nine, um."

"When sewing on the buttons - HOW MANY stitches

through each pair of holes?"

"Six, um."

"And HOW do we fasten off?"

Our combined attention was constantly tested. Yet if anyone's mind strayed, the chorusing answer would rouse them.

Mending was given the same conscientious tuition: darning and patching charted with pencil and paper before we set hand near the fabric. Our patches were turned to a tailor's precision and our darns were designs to be proud of.

In knitting, we learnt the art of turning the heel of a sock, shaping the toe of a sock, and fashioning the leg - of a sock, all in short practice pieces, always in the same red or green practice knitting cotton. Inspired, I began a pair of real socks for Dad in my home time. But both of his feet could have got inside the first completed sock - so I gave up. But the heel, and the toe, and the shaping were beautifully fashioned!

"Ah, well," Dad sympathised. "You'n get the 'ang on it when you'n had a bit more practice."

Needlework did not stop with the mundane. Presents for mothers at Christmas were embroidered, be they aprons, peg-bags, table-runners, chairbacks, ovencloths, or traycloths. Sometimes the Mistress brought along work of her own which she set us to.

One particular set was the loveliest job I ever sewed. It arrived with ink-coloured thistle outlines on natural-coloured linen. They were in the corners of dinner-place mats, table-napkins and a large centre cloth. The set was to be a wedding-present for somebody special. We separated strands of silky cotton and followed each line of each thistle flower with light and springy stem stitches. There were shades of pinks and mauves and deeper purply colours and strong-soft greens for the leaves and the spikes. It was THE loveliest thing to sew the life into them.

They looked real enough to smell and to stroke them. They began my lasting love of thistle flowers. There is something at once bold and fragile about them, their spikes and their silky softness together.

When sewing proceeded quietly and no one needed help, that was when the Mistress indulged us with snippets of news. We heard about goings-on at the Women's Institute, like who won the competitions. I never met Mrs Tanner, but she was an impressive lady, for the Mistress spoke so highly of her.

She told us about family happenings and family holidays, and about Yorkshire; and about their grown-up daughter, who "went to Number Ten Downing Street to have tea with Mrs Ramsay MacDonald!"

Plans for future sewing lessons, happenings round about, thoughts about our own futures and when she and the Master would retire, what our parents thought - or should have thought - about this or that event of national news, all reached our heads bowed over stitching.

And it was at sewing-time that I remember our being handed slim magazines with blue lettering on slippery white pages. They had pictures of serious-looking people, all with hazy grey faces.

"Tell your parents," the Mistress said, "to read this magazine. And tell them I hope they will be sure to vote for Mr Duckworth!"

I don't think she actually said, "Woe betide ...", yet I have a feeling that perhaps it was meant to be implied.

Woe Betide

Chapter Seven

Weasles and Things

Whenever the children - or the animal Bruin Boys in comics - had measles, they became covered instantly, dramatically, with brilliant red spots. Mine were not a bit like that.

It was a Friday morning, right at the end of February. I made my sleepy steps downstairs. Mum was holding the enamel jug beneath the tap in the side of the firegrate. She carried it steaming into the back kitchen, and emptied it into the bowl.

"Take your nighty off," she said, "and be sure to wash your neck thoroughly. You can come in by the fire to dry - it's perishing this morning."

Soap made cloudy strands through the clear water. As my hands carried the warmth over me, I shivered. The cold I'd gone to bed with the night before felt nasty in my throat. Mum handed me the towel, warm from the line over the fireplace, and I spluttered something between a cough and a sneeze. Then again. She gave me a look, and a closer look, from my face to my neck and over the rest of me.

"Oh, no!" she said. "You can't get dressed for school. Just look at this! You've got the measles!"

I looked and wondered how she could tell. Because my spots were not big, or bright red, but had tiny centres. I could hardly tell them from gooseflesh - they were sort of transparent, like when snowflakes first land and you can still see the ground through the spread of them.

"Get your nighty back on, and get by the fire in the rocking-chair. I'll fetch a blanket to go round you for now."

When Dot called for me, she was given a message

for school.

"It's not surprising, I suppose," was Dot's comment." There's a lot on 'em about. Both the girls at the farm 'ave got 'em. I've had 'em already." Dot was, after all, one of the big girls.

Whilst the door was open, flakes of snow blew in, and rested on the red floortiles.

"Quite a covering on the path," Mum said. "It's soon come on. It was as clear as anything when Dad went off for six o'clock. And what a wind! I shouldn't think Dot ought to go - it's hardly fit."

From my blanket in the chair, I could see the snow fly in a fury past the window. So quickly it moved that it didn't look like snow at all - more like handfuls of chalklines all scibbled along fast together.

Mum set about warming my bedroom. She pulled the heavy iron shelf from the middle of the oven on the far side of the fireplace. With a piece of old sheeting and a length of bindertwine, she packed it into a flat parcel, and took it up to warm the bed. She trimmed the wick of the dumpy paraffin stove and carried that upstairs.

"We'll let it warm up a bit," she said, "and then you'll have to go back to bed."

There was a strange white gloom in the back kitchen when I walked through to the stairs. The window was coated to most of its depth with mounting snow. Flakes were landing fast against the glass, spreading themselves, as they fell nearly filling the whole of the window's panes.

At dinner-time Dad was told of my measles.

"I thought last night 'er was sicknin' for summat," was his response. "'Er didna look right about the eyes somehow."

"I'n call and ask 'em at the farm to ring up Doctor Gittins when I get back. Mind you, he wunna come today, sure not to. He conna get out of Cressage, I doubt. Ee, the roads is terrible. Never see'd anything like this, never in all my life any road up. I reckon owd Nick isself is driving that wind. You just hark at it, surree!"

So it came about that the blizzard of 1933 vented its fury on the day of that Friday, while the measles forced its own pace through me. And so it came about that my memories of both are inseparable.

There are memories of nice things, like hot blackcurrant tea made from jam, and the smooth, grainy feel and the smoky flowerdust sweetness of honey, bit hard from the spoon. Under the howl of the wind and the white lashings past the window, was a comfortable feeling through my fever of *The Thatch* being wrapped round in a blanket. There was the glow of the oil-heater, and the warm, sweet smell of it, unfamiliar in the bedroom, as dusk fell, and Mum saying that everyone's meat and bread would be getting as far as *The Horseshoe,* and left there for somebody to fetch with the farmhorses. (Farmhorses could get through snowfilled lanes better than anything.)

A flood over the white sheet from my sudden nosebleed mingled in my mind with blood on the snow in a fairytale.

In the evening, I was allowed downstairs. Tucked up on the sofa, shading my eyes from the fire's heat, I drowsed through conversations all about blizzards and measles, and things connected.

I croaked a laugh when Dad told of his visit to the farmhouse after dinner, when "Young George" sought him excitedly asking, "Has Sene really got the weasles now, Mr Farlow?"

"The sheep and the lambs have had to be put in the stackyard. Making an eck of a mess of the turmit humps, but it canna be helped. It's the only thing to do. There's even a tuthree lambs in the farm's back kitchen."

"What about all them little chicks I saw last week?" Mum asked.

"They'n had to be put in the carthouse. I doubt if many of 'em'll survive. They'n be starved to dyeth, there inna much on em to keep 'emselves warm."

"It ketches folks off their guard when it comes as late as this. It was real nice weather most of January, remember them warm days we had? Almost like summer. Then there was that sharp frost at the end when they had to put the Ploughing Match off. But we had a lovely day for it the week after - and for the coursing. We'n all bin thinking winter was getting on for over - and now this."

"They say the streets is blocked in Soosbry. Conna get up the Cop anyway - filled right up. It's the roads and the lanes 'as got it worst. Not all that much snow on the fields, considering. The owd wind's lifted it over the hedges into drifts on the roads."

The snow stopped falling with the dark on Friday. People began to take stock and dig out buried cars and things on Saturday. More snow fell on Sunday, but by Monday it turned to rain and the earth was bound again, this time by water.

But we went on talking about the blizzard. Everyone said it was once in a lifetime. Even the oldest ones said there had been nothing like it before. Everyone had drama to relate from wherever they had been at the time, and the tales took a while to get round.

There were tales of lorry-drivers, stuck in the lanes, who stepped out of their cabins - then found themselves up to the chin in snow.

And of people who plodded over snow-hidden field-tracks to find their gateway to the lane blocked by towering white shapes, sculpted by the wind into petrified monsters.

Hearses got stuck taking coffins to funerals. One in Ismore Lane and another on Cronkhill Bank. Horses and carts eventually shifted them, but the funerals had to wait. People were said to have left their homes on that Friday, not returning till the middle of the next week.

Donnington School was closed the following week. The blizzard had been especially bad down Donnington Lane. People told how the Master had carried little ones, one under each arm, through the drifts to the safety of the bottom road. It took several journeys and he was exhausted. Everyone said how kind and how brave the Master had been.

By the time I was able to go to school again the excitement was over and they were singing songs about daffodils. In the meantime my measles followed its course of days in bed with goosefat rubbed into my chest for the cough; and of sleepy evenings down on the sofa. Through half-shut, measly-sore eyes I watched as Mum did her ironing, and her sewing. And I watched Dad put the poker into the fire, leaving it there a while. Then he pulled it out red-hot and plunged it steaming and spluttering into his mug of beer.

Lulled by the warmth and their voices, becoming more distant, from that mystery-land between waking and sleeping, feeling myself lifted, I heard Dad's whisper – "Er's dropped off. Open the door for us, oot, and I'n carry 'er up."

Chapter 8

Number Six: Window Seat

In the summer, whilst I was seven, we moved to Number Six, Uckington. I'm not sure why. Perhaps my mother was still bothered about *The Thatch,* perhaps about the way over the field, the blizzard having been the last straw - perhaps. The lane went all the way to Number Six. There were so many different things for a child to enjoy.

Luthers lived at Number Five, and their garden flanked the shared front path. They had masses of flowers I had never seen close-up, like lilies, moss-roses, Canterbury Bells, and great rich cushions of spicy pinks - clumps of Sweet William - oh, and a whole lot more whose names I never did learn. The end of their house was covered by a pear-tree, fanned against the wall.

Our house was joined to the back of the Luthers'. We faced the main road, though still more than a field away. No thatch this time, but we had diamond panes in the windows, like picture-book cottages. Our diamonds had smudgy corners, for it was hard to get your fingers right in to the corners to clean them, and there were so many panes, and, Mum said, too many corners in a whole window.

Inside, the house seemed spacious. This front door opened into a hall-way which led through to the back kitchen. The proper kitchen was to the left of the hall. On the right, immediately behind the front door was the staircase. It seemed so wide and high, having no stairs door. The walls went right up to the upstairs ceiling. The hollowness filled with echoes of every footstep, every voice, every whispered word, and every creak from the brown, uncarpeted steps. Halfway up, the steps changed direction to the landing. The landing itself was almost a little room, with its own window looking Wrekinwards. The big metal box stood under the window. Inside it were our best clothes. The smell of camphor and lavender spread through the house when the box was open.

I sat often on the landing-box, its pattern digging into my legs. I liked that place to read, and the world in the book could merge with whatever my fancy wove round the view from the window. Red and pink roses climbed round the front door and upwards round the landing window.

Beyond our front garden and the row of gooseberry bushes, was a solid hawthorn hedge where blackbirds and thrushes and hedgesparrows nested. A path round the back led to three stone pigsties. As with the houses, ours was the middle one. From around mid-summer to Christmas it was the pig's, but earlier in the year it could be mine. It could become my own pretend house, but best of all it became a shop.

Neighbours on both sides, as well as Mum, saved empty grocery-tins and packets. Wooden orange boxes became a counter, covered with a cloth so that I could keep things underneath it. More boxes made shelves to be filled with, apparently, Golden Syrup, Quaker Oats, Force, Cherry Blossom and Mansion polish, Rinso, Sunlight Soap, Black Bell tobacco, Black Cat cigarettes. Mum even handed me blue sugar-bags and pink sultana-bags to fill with earth or stones to their original shape. Mum always loved a reason not to throw things away.

Joan and Barbara made a shop in one of the farm pigsties. One enterprising day, we all went to Norton Shop to ask Mrs Stephenson for any advertisements she no longer used, or anything at all, we said, which would make our shops look more real, please. She found us a bundle of self-standing pictures of lipsticked ladies with tightly permed hair - and a sackful of whitish packets with green labels and Lyon's Tea printed along their sides. She had just turned out her window, and she said these were 'dummy' packets. Thus we learned that things in shop-windows were not always as they seemed. We hauled the treasure home and shared it out. We were each working in semi-secrecy, until the formal opening and mutual inspection of our respective shops.

I can still see the girls' faces, their brown eyes shining as they stepped under the stone arch from the sunlight. They peered around and sniffed.

"Oh, Sene!" said Barbara. "Yours really smells like a proper shop!"

Before the pigsties was a low wall, with little creeping plants between its stones. Topped with iron hurdles, it contained the stockyard with an old wooden barn. Between that and the main road lay the Big Field.

Always pasture land, this field had a number of little ridges, not hills, but enough to be fun when we ran among them. In summer we could sit in its folds for our talking games, make daisy-chains - test who liked butter with buttercups. And we could see over into the lane, and watch to greet people expected from the bus, or wave them on their way again. It was a happy field, light in spirit as were our feet when we picked its wildflowers, peered into its birds-nests, or sang our songs under its skylarks, and as we ran and we rolled among its ridges and hollows.

Over to the left, out of view from the window-seat, was the beginning of a brook. One of the field's hollows was joined by an outburst of water from what we called a spring, though it came along underground in an earthenware pipe. It spurted forth through an iron grating, frothing into the ditch and ploughing itself a way among the pebbles. Then turning, it forged for itself ways between the waterplants into a steady stream under the hedge, through *The Patch* field by the Taylors', touching the farthest corner of their garden, and into the ditch along the Back Lane to ... wherever.

We filled buckets at the spring for the drinking

water-steen in the pantry. Only one field and a lane's width away this was a different world altogether from that other - sinister – water-place from which Ginny Greenteeth reigned. This was a world for water-nymphs, with daisy-petal tiaras, to tip their flimsy toes on the cress.

At school we had been learning a poem about a brook. The Master had been talking with us about the words for the sounds that the water made. Here I had my own, a living model, and I felt the Tennyson man had caught my little stream in his poem. And his was the first poem to have meaning as a poem for me.

There was no trout in our brook - but, once a frog leapt, all yellow and slippery, from an armful of wet leaves one Saturday morning when Joan and I were playing at making a dam. We made up a sort of song about him:

"Poor old Froggy! Poor old Froggy!
Poor old Froggy Woggy Doodle!"

We sang it for ages all around the farm, but nobody else knew where the song came from.

A few feet from the landing window-seat was the place for a game to be played, privately, when the house was otherwise empty, by myself, with the echoey walls. By now, I had a copy of the Prayer Book. We sang practice church services at school, with the Master taking the part of the Vicar. Half-way down the top stretch of steps, high enough for light from the window, yet low enough to make the most of the echoes, I sat. The echoes and I began with the Confirmation Service, continually in rehearsal at school. We celebrated Morning and Evening Prayer, the Solemnisation of Matrimony, the Baptism of Infants and worked our way through the liturgical year, with collects and readings and hymns. I kept my voice clear and controlled for the Vicar, and flowed with all the resonance I could muster, for the echoes to chant back their responses. Hymns had the benefit of Sundays, when Joan's Grandad Evans took us to chapel, where he was sometimes preacher. The point here is that I had learnt to sing hymns with a full 'chapel' heart. All of this went into my church on the stairs – and all the voices of my echo-choirs sang them with me.

Kitchens

Kitchens go with cooking - in nineteen-thirties Uckington farm cottages therefore, the kitchen was still where the fireplace was, and where almost every indoor activity - bar sleeping - also happened. Some cottages had a back-kitchen as well for dirtiest jobs like skinning and gutting an occasional rabbit, or plucking a chicken. The back-kitchen table might have an enamel bowl and the soap dish for family face and hands washing. Sometimes there was a separate wash-house with a built-in brick washing boiler, its wooden lid well steeped with soapy steam, and with its fireplace underneath, and there was the mangle and the corrugated aluminium dolly-tub and the dolly which looked like a squat wooden stool on a long handle. At *The Thatch* we had a back kitchen and a wash-house, but at Number Six all these things, as well as Dad's bicycle lived in the back kitchen. The words 'scullery' and 'living-room' , along with 'ironing-board', as I came to know them, belonged in town houses.

It was long after we left Uckington that even a cold tap became usual in country cottages. Even when council houses began to arrive in the countryside, with fixed baths in bathrooms, running water was not always deemed necessary for their use. Many did not get proper plumbing until the 1950s or later. But, of course, I cannot speak for Uckington for we left in 1938.

Along with the fireplace, the kitchen-table was the hub of family life, from and to which all else related. As well as being where all meals were eaten it was where everything which was eaten was prepared: pastry rolled on its wooden board, cakes mixed, jam potted, beans sliced, peas hulled - and crocks washed up and drained on to a tray. Clothes were cut out there, sewn together there, ironed and mended on its white wooden top, untreated but for scrubbing. Something of the table's seasoned finish could well have been residual soapsuds, ironed in over years.

Ironing, as well as cooking, needed the fire and the table. We covered the top with several layers of old blanket and as many layers of once white sheeting. By now the sheet's function shewed in variegated shades of scorched iron-shapes, strewn like autumn leaves over its worn surface.

The fire had to be stoked up well in advance, with coals to above the level of the front bars. Flames must mature to a gleedy radiant heat, for smoke would ruin everything. When all was glowing, a support for the irons was set in place. Sometimes that was part of the grate, sometimes a rack fitted as needed. Done too soon, this would 'draw out' the smoke into the room. At least two irons were used, turn about. They were surprisingly small - not a lot bigger than a hand, for they needed to be handled quickly and surely. With a thick padded holder, usually one made at school, a hot iron was lifted. Its scorching surface was deftly flipped against an old duster, probably one of Dad's old shirts. The iron was held close to the face to judge the heat: a froth of spit sent sizzling along its surface confirmed it ready. A reluctant steamy dribble meant back to the fire for a bit longer.

Confident strokes, smoothing the pleats and the flares and the gathers, had to make the most possible progress before the heat went. 'Hard' collars and shirt fronts had extra treatment. Dad liked his collars soft, but I had watched my Granma rubbing their collars and cuffs and shirt fronts with a starch block, almost like a thick stubby candle. After the starch's first pressing in, the iron all but skated over the polished surface.

Housekeeping in the lean years needs special prudence with expensive resources. At one and eightpence a bag for cobbles, coal took a chunk from a meagre budget. So baking or roasting could be going on in the oven to make fullest use of the extra firing.

Prim garments and crisply folded linen hung around. Cord, or wire clothes lines were strung along and under the mantelpiece and over the room, between picture hooks or on their own special nails. The kitchen was alive with fragrance blended of fresh-air and soap lifted at the irons' smoothing heat, and the smells seeping from the oven, it teased the nose and touched the face as you wove a way between dresses and shirts and sheets and towels.

Housekeeping was hard work in those days. Be she mother, or aunty, or grandmother, or whoever, a housekeeper with beacon face and breaking back, before anyone thought of a word for 'job satisfaction' or 'productivity' - she lived them both, without obvious question. With dextrous hands, and what must have been intuitive organisation, she simply got on with it.

To the sounds of sizzling from the oven, or the singing kettle from the hob, of an occasional fluttering from the subsiding fire, the last warmth persuaded into the last crease, she lifted the kettle into the coals to splutter to the boil. She reached the caddy from the mantelpiece, made some tea, and sat for the shortest of rests before the next job.

Back Garden

The back kitchen-window at Number Six looked towards the main vegetable garden. But first was a yard - a patch trodden hard enough for etching hopscotch squares, bare earth hedged here and there with tufts of grass and the odd brick and stone. On the corner of the house near the back door was the rainwater tub where I met all sorts of wriggly water insects. We used the water for everything except drinking and cooking. In the opposite corner, sharing a wall with the house, was the WC. We were, I supposed, becoming modernised (?) for here we had a hinged seat and a bucket, not quite so mysterious as *The Thatch's* earth closet. Yet, all credit to my parents' discretion, I never knew where the bucket was emptied every few days, though I came to know that enormous garden very well indeed.

At the far edge of the small yard, opposite the window, stood a tall, dilapidated wooden shed, only the width of its door. Probably it was held together by the elder roots at its base and the ivy which laced its breaking sides. We called it the hovel. And because I liked it so much, tucked as it was among the bushes and the evergreens, I grew up believing that 'hovel' was a word for something nice. Our hovel housed long strips of weathered wood, waiting to be chopped for firing, and long handled garden tools. Everything had to be stacked upwards where the space was. In its highest corners spiders lived with their pantry webs, and bits of one-time hay where birds had nested. It was by the hovel, among the tangled mass of ivy and things, that I first saw a wren. But I never saw its nest.

The back garden was large, and very roughly triangular, with a long low hedge along the lane. A short boundary with Number Five, and a longer one with Number Seven, met with our house at the hopscotch yard. Damson trees stood in the hedges like measuring-marks and apple trees were sprinkled over the garden.

The hedge between us and Number Seven had a bend, so you could not see all of our garden at once. At the bend was an apple tree stump and my favourite damson tree. They grew out of a small patch I'd been given to dig and to grow seeds for myself. How I longed and I worked for that to be like Luthers' pathside garden, but mine got stuck on Virginia Stock with petals like dolly-mixtures, with daisy-faced marigolds and pinky clarkia – all right as far as they went. But I wondered what were the secrets which added up to the difference between those erratic spots of colour and the glory of those borders along the front path.

But a glory of my own I did have. I found it one Sunday morning in fullest spring. It was one of those mornings when the sun was impatient to get the world moving again, almost before people had got to sleep after their Saturday night.

Its earliest light reflected from my open window, and it reached me at about the same time as the first tentative twittering. Gradually the birdsong built up. Blackbirds, thrushes, chaffinches, sparrows - and more - millions of them it seemed - coo-curled along by the pigeons and called over the top by the cuckoo, lambs bleating and rumble-answers from their mothers in the field down the lane. And I was awake so early on a Sunday morning - no one else would be about for hours.

I found my book between the bed and wall where it fell the night before. But this was no time to be indoors. I quickly dressed, then carrying the book and my shoes, trod as quietly as I could down the creaky echoey stairs. Rainwater from the tub in the enamel bowl, with the new tablet of soap from last night's bath, the letters still showing, was fresh and flowery over my face. A quick dry - and out into this sparkling and chorusing day - new and quite perfect, like a present still half in its wrapper, untouched and mysterious. Something fluttered as I passed the wren's place in the hovel's ivy, but mostly the performance went on as though I was not there. The damson trees were in full bloom and the sun lit up diamond reflections, like when frost sparkles on snowdrifts.

At the place where I'd sown the flower seeds, packets on twigs marking the rows, patches of earth were still showing dark from the night's watering. Balancing, one foot at a time on my pebble pathway, I reached the foot of the damson tree. It was my favourite partly because of the way the branches grew, starting high enough and low enough for me to climb. I could grasp a strong branch, my shoe in a good foothold, and swing up and around into the cradle of branches, then up again, higher into the seat place. I was always too plump to be athletic, but this was a climb within my limits, even carrying a book and yet it led me to another world ... Here I could come, and sit, and I could read ... or sit and dream.

But on this day, at this time, in this sunlight, amid such music and in such company, I simply looked and I listened and I grew in experience. This was the nearest to heaven, I had been - ever. I could not imagine anything more beautiful. I have said that the damson trees in blossom were like snowdrifts. Well, up in my tree it was different in this way: as a single snowflake, or even thousands of separate snowflakes compare with drifted snow, so a single damson flower, or even millions of separate damson flowers seen from inside, among the tree's branches compares with drifts of blossom seen from the path. These tiny single blooms were basically white, but with tiny veined flecks. This powerful morning sunlight shone through the fragile substance of each petal of each single flower. I peered at the millions of them against a sky the colour of sparrows' eggs. I watched the mysterious underside of bees as they peered from their sky side before entering the tiny blooms to taste and see.

There have been many times when my heart has sung in praise to the Creator . Once in a while though, the tremendous richness has so impressed itself as to become a part of me, a kind of personal 'bench-mark' in sensibility . This was one of those – the stuff, I now feel, of which psalms could have been born.

The house was quiet and cave-like by contrast. Farmers and waggoners shared Sunday feeding of the horses and this was a morning off for Dad. I felt like some tea - and wouldn't that surprise them?

Quietly as I could, I raked out the cinders and the dust from the ess-hole and the flues; a few big sheets of newspaper, lightly crushed in my hands and set into the fireplace to be criss-crossed with sticks. Mum always put the sticks to dry in the oven over-night for a quick start. It took a lot of sticks right up to the level where I placed the kettle on the top bar of grating. Small cobbles of coal were next, perched lightly around the kettle. One match was enough to set alight a number of fluted points of newsprint. I liked to watch the frilly grey edges as the flames ate up the words and pictures of last week's news.

The skill in this kind of fire-lighting lay in keeping enough heat from sticks and paper to get the kettle at least singing and lively before the coals took over. The kettle settled into the space of the vanishing sticks, then the coals well started, fell into place while I made the tea. We learnt about the theory of fire lighting at school, for it was one of our recurring topics for compositions - we knew it by heart.

The cups of tea I took for Mum and Dad didn't look quite as when Mum made it, but they were pleased. I shovelled the cinders into the bucket to be riddled for banking the fire after breakfast, and set about keeping a good fire for the bacon. I left the frying to Mum. Dad never liked bacon smoked by whatever means.

My Friend, Hilda

Numbers Five, Six and Seven Uckington stood together, but each was quite different from the others. We were joined on to Luthers' but Number Seven, Taylors' was separate. You could walk all round their house.

The front path which ran between Luthers' flowerbeds continued in a straight line past the fronts of our house and Taylors', to the *Patch* field on the way to the water-spring. Taylors' had a rose which rambled its red flowers round their front door. Between that and their back door was a brilliant pink Japonica with gold dust in its centres. It was the first Japonica I'd seen and every summer followed on its waxy flowers.

Facing our back door, and my bedroom window, over the gardens between us, Taylors' house had a small window at the foot of their stairs, and another above it to a landing room which was Hilda's. An apple or a pear tree fanned out its branches against the shape of their side wall.

I spent a lot of time at the Taylors'. Their large family had by now grown up. Two at least, of the sons were policemen, and all but the youngest children, twin girls, had left home.

Bertha was beautiful. Her dark hair was rich with waves neatly fastened round her rosy face. Her eyes were warm and brown, and her figure full, not at all fat, but rounded, like the whole of her. She must have been everyone's ideal of country healthiness. Eventually Bertha went to work, for a Master at Prestfelde School. This meant 'living-in'. And then there was one: Hilda.

Hilda was at home, almost always. She and I were especially good friends, although she was quite ten years older than me. She was not taller.

Often Hilda stood by the open back door, her arm raised, supporting herself on the doorpost. There the sunlight found her hair, smooth and dark, shining it like autumn chestnuts. She too had happy brown eyes. Her face, longer in shape than her sister's, told a sallow story of much of her life spent out of the sun's reach. She had a heavier jaw-line than Bertha too, and her bottom lip became indented with the forward line of her teeth, when she strained over such effort as she needed to walk.

Her full height was shortened by the curve of her back, with muscular shoulders that bore the burden of her movement. Crutches stood within her reach, but indoors, she chose to get around supported by the furniture and doorposts. Her knuckles shone white through their skin as she gripped the edge of solid things.

Her body leaned this way and that, as her legs jerked obediently after her. Leather straps of full length calipers wheezed and the metal side pieces made their own rattle. The effort made her pant, and yet she stopped for a laugh, often when she saw something to amuse her. She found humour in the least likely places. She was quite beside herself when she began to giggle. Then a deep breath, and she was away again.

"A-a-ah-well! I must get on," she said. I never once saw her miserable or irritable.

A combination of crutches, walking-sticks and a wheelchair meant she could occasionally go out. But outings were infrequent, and at most a walk as far as the lane on a summer evening, or in the wheelchair a bit further, for her father and mother were quite elderly compared with my parents, so mostly Hilda was at home. Sometimes she knocked on their window, and beckoned me.

"C-can you come in on Saturday morning? Our Mum wants to go to town."

"Yes, I 'spect I can. I'd better check with my Mum. What time shall I come?"

"C-come early. Then we'll have longer to do things."

We often kept each other company when either or sometimes both of our mothers went into Shrewsbury on the bus. Hilda was able to wash up, peel potatoes, shell peas, top and tail gooseberries and such jobs, we did them together. Some days she was cleaning cutlery and ornaments with rag dusters, and a tin of Silvo. Often she was knitting, in her corner seat by the fireplace. We both did 'French knitting' over four rivets fixed into a cotton reel. Even when we started off together, her bright woolly snake grew much more quickly than mine. Sometimes we were unpicking old things to get more wool.

We looked at picture-books together, at encyclopaedia books, magazines, anything with pictures. Sometimes I read stories from my books. I tried hard to teach Hilda to read, but I was a poor teacher. But, most of all, whatever else we were doing at the same time, she told me stories.

Most of her childhood had been spent at *Park Hall* – the name she used for the orthopaedic hospital near 'Ossestry'. Her tales were of pranks played in the Children's Ward, and of how Sister asserted her authority and restored order. My favourite books from our school library were school stories, about midnight picnics and escapades in dormitories and so on. So I responded well to Hilda's adventures, brought to life by she who had actually taken part!

"Laws, Sene!" she laughed. "We did'n 'alf have some fun! You'd never believe the things we did!"

I learned about the merits, shortcomings and eccentricities of this Sister, or that Nurse, or the other Doctor. And she told me vividly what she remembered about the operations she'd had , and they were many. I held my breath as she told me about the chloroform pad which put her to sleep. To this day I have a horror of things over my face.

In ordinary conversation she was restricted by a severe stammer, but when she launched into her stories, we forgot all about the stammer.

Hilda's family were all kind to me. When she went to town Mrs Taylor always brought me a cone-shaped white paper bag full of dark chocolate snapped into pieces, with crisp white 'cream' filling. Bertha took me on the bus to the pictures in Wellington on her days off. They had a wireless long before we did and we were invited in to listen to *'In Town Tonight'*, or *'Henry Hall's Guest Night'*. Once we went in to hear a programme about Gracie Fields. Dad bought a Gracie record one Saturday when he went into town for some boots. Ours was called *'In the Chapel in the Moonlight'*, and I thought her sweet voice must be how angels sang. But to sit in Taylors' house and hear Gracie not only singing, but laughing and speaking in a Lancashire accent I had never heard, was magic.

On our mornings together, we heard the Daily Service on the wireless. When I told Mum the man had said it was from Birmingham, she said that was where my Aunty Nance lived – "Did you hear her singing?"

Mum's remark had an effect she could not have intended. For the next fifty or so years, whenever I heard the Daily Service, with the distinctive sound of the BBC Singers, one picture always came to mind. It was of about four or five ladies in an otherwise empty church, each of them looking exactly as Aunty Nance did in a picture we had of her taken some years before then. Each of them wore her high cloche hat, almost covering their eyes, and every one of them wore a sepia-coloured,(then fashionable) shapeless coat.

A few years ago now there was a picture in the *Radio Times* of the BBC Singers. I was astonished, for they were young: men in evening suits, women in pretty white dresses, modern hairstyles - not a cloche hat to be seen! And they looked a lot less serious than Aunty Nance in her photograph.

Hilda and I kept up our friendship for a few years after the Uckington ones, but eventually we lapsed. Sadly, she died at Beeches Hospital, about the time I was planning to move back to Shropshire. I wish I'd come back sooner.

Dignity and Depression

Hilda and her family have an important part in my picture of the nineteen thirties not least because that time was called 'The Depression'.

All of the houses around Uckington farm were 'tied' cottages. It follows that people living in them worked on the farm. Dad was waggoner, so was Mr. Luther; Joanie's Dad, Mr. Beedles, was cowman; Mr. Pugh was shepherd, Mr. Wainwright, pigman; Mr. Jack Lewis, who followed us into *The Thatch*, and a younger Tommy Habberley were involved with tractors and machinery. Through the darkest years of the national recession, all these men had work and weekly wages, though there was a time when the actual amount went down.

Mr Taylor no longer had regular work. Perhaps it was that, being older he was less fit - or perhaps he had been hurt in the war, I really don't know. Hilda's Grandad Mason had died while we were still at *The Thatch*. He had worked at Uckington farm until a very old man. It used to be said that he could remember his father ploughing at Uckington with a team of bullocks, and that he himself had worked as a child with donkeys at Wheathill Farm.

But now there was work for Mr Taylor only at busiest seasons, beet hoeing, beet pulling, harvesting and so on. Then it was 'piece' work, paid for as needed, and nothing in between. So he cycled to other farms looking for 'casual' work. When there was none, he still cycled - all the way to town to the Labour Exchange. Farm workers were not included in the general national insurance arrangements, so I'm not sure that he would have received dole money.

He trod past our window many times and most days. A smallish figure, I picture him in a sandy-coloured coat, with sandy-grey hair showing under his trilby hat. He pushed a tall bicycle with orange handle grips. It was on his regular Friday journey to the Labour Exchange that Mum gave her sigh – "Poor Mr Taylor."

I could never have understood all that it meant. There was a lot in the papers about what they called 'The Depression'. There was a lot about hardship and dole queues in the big towns, and about factories being closed. I did not know much about factories, though I had seen the smoke over the fields from the sugarbeet one at Allscott. That was only ever open through the winter months anyway. We heard hooters from the Sentinel, checked our clocks by them. Mum said that was a factory, but I didn't really know what it did.

I certainly could not imagine life in a town, depressed or not. But I could see the reality of Mr Taylor's share in 'The Depression' - and I could feel that it mattered as Mum sighed "Poor Mr Taylor." I could feel, because of the sort of person she was, that something of her went with him in compassion, and thence to his wife and to Hilda. Through them, Mum told me. Through them, she sympathised, and cared about the distress of those times. And I knew that it mattered, because of how she cared.

It was not so much a matter of money poverty. A large grown-up family would not let parents want. The sadness had more to do with the spirit - with the indignity of rejection - with not being valued enough as a person to be regularly wanted. Still more, it had to do with a man having time on his hands - enough time to recognise the indignity, and to brood about it.

For I remember the hours which Dad and the others worked. Dad worked the clock round as a matter of course every weekday, only a little less in deepest winter. At the peak of summer he worked all daylight hours and even into the reluctant high summer twilight at haymaking - and again at corn harvest.

Of those hours - I now understand - about fifty or perhaps fifty-four were counted as the basic week, paid for with around thirty one shillings, with a few shillings more when the man was responsible for animals. The rest were counted as overtime at something like ninepence an hour. Actual wages would vary from farm to farm, so with free milk, manure for the garden, rent and other such considerations. These were a matter of arrangement between each farmer and his workers: some allowed them, some did not.

It is when I remember the interminable hours and the exhaustion - and the frustration, especially when the wage went down - that I find myself wanting to ask again about dignity and work, and to reconsider the meaning of it. If there was a dignity for those workers then, it surely came of not having the time to think about it.

Many farmworkers resisted calls to join the Union of Agricultural Workers. They would not risk losing the farmers' goodwill. For loss of favour might mean loss of the job, and consequently the home that went with it. Dad got cross at the very word 'Union'. He regarded it with great suspicion and refused to consider joining.

The farmers' own union protested against any compulsory increase in wage rates. They said they were paying wages out of capital as it was. Hard times in the towns brought down food prices. The harder those in the countryside worked the more food they produced - and the cheaper it had to be sold. So farm incomes went down as their effort went up.

Another factor in the farmers' budgeting was pressure towards higher standards, particularly with regard to milk supply. Roadside hedges began to sprout notices which announced 'Grade A', indicating standards of hygiene at that particular farm. Then the letters 'T T Herd' were added, telling those in the know that those cows had been tested and treated against Tuberculosis. That meant that, wherever else the passer-by might pick up T B, it could not be from milk produced at that particular farm. And all that cost the farmers money.

Eventually pasteurisation became compulsory, and milk never tasted the same again. But nor did it carry what had been one of life's closest hazards.

Our family was fortunate that we were not really ever-so-hungry-poor, as some bigger families were. My stocky shape confirmed that I, at any rate, had what I needed to eat.

"Er dunna crack many deaf nuts! - by the look on er," grown-ups used to say of me. If there were any "deaf nuts" in our family diet, I know now who would have kept them to herself, that the rest of us should not want.

The pantry at Number Six was the nicest I have ever known, light and fresh and roomy, with lots of lovely shelves. Yet... Mum bought only from week to week. Apart from the year's jam and stone-jars of salted kidney beans, there was not a lot to put on the shelves.

What we bought in town had, of course, to be paid for there and then. But we had changed our baker. Dad had turned against Morris's bread. He claimed it no longer "satisfied".

"By middle-morning you'm as clemmed as if you'n ad none."

So now Mr Birch came twice a week from Rodington. Each time we handed him a list of groceries to bring at the next visit.

"How many loaves today Mrs Farlow?"

"I'd better have four - and have you got a stale one, please?"

Mr Birch added up the bill, while I breathed in the lovely bread smell. At the very hardest times, if the bill came to, say eighteen shillings and sixpence, Mum might say, "Would you mind taking fifteen this time please?" - or whatever she could manage.

"That's all right. Thank you very much," replied Mr Birch and he did a take away sum on the bill. He was kind. And he knew, and we knew, that the Christmas pig, or the harvest money, or less certainly, the damsons, could be relied upon to wipe the slate clean. Then we'd buy something extra for a treat - perhaps a couple of Chelseas for Mum and Dad - and for me, one of those crinkly shortcakes in a paper case with powdery sugar and a dollop of red jelly on top. I loved those.

Chapter Nine

SHREWSBURY SATURDAYS

The Bus into Town

Most Saturday mornings were for Shrewsbury - or Shrosebury - Shoosbury - Soosbury - or sometimes even Sollop (Salop), then, as now, depending entirely on how one happens to feel about it.

Mum and I often went together, though sometimes she left me with Hilda, or at the farm and went alone. Occasionally, if Mum was not well, or was especially hard pressed, either for money or time, she sent me, under the caring eye of Joanie's Granny Beedles – "Just see that she gets on and off the bus at the right place, please, then she'll be all right," Mum said. And I was given money and a shopping-list.

Whichever contingency, it meant a scant and hurried breakfast. I never understood why anything as bland as plain bread and margarine first thing in the morning left such a strange distinctive after-taste. It didn't happen at any other time of day.

We waited, or ran, for the bus at the Horse Shoe Garage, or at the lane end from Number Six. We climbed up among the baskets. Everybody had a basket, sturdy and square or tub-shaped, some with gingham or white covers, which meant they held things to be sold at the Market. You could only guess whether a spike poking up the cover was a rabbit's foot or a kidney bean. Everyone was secretive about what the baskets held. Even when a cloth was raised to slip in a purse, you never even glimpsed the contents. When we took things from the garden, Mum was just the same – "We don't need to make everybody else as wise as ourselves!" - her phrase to cover such a situation. Mum's vocabulary was made up of her fitting phrases.

"One and a half to the Square please." Her red ticket cost sixpence and my blue one threepence.

We picked up more people at Norton Cross Roads and again at Ismore Lane end, and more at Atcham.

"Oh dear! Something's run into the bridge – again!" was a frequent cry as we rounded the bend in the road over the first river. Over the broken ridge, down through the trees and the overhanging shrubs, the River Tern twinkled its own tale.

Beyond the next bridge, at Atcham, the Severn trailed through a field. Cows grazed along its banks, drank it, and even stood soaking their feet. Other times fishermen sat or stood, living distantly along their lines.

Before the rise which was Emstrey Bank, what began as a field was churned up, spread about, and gradually transformed over weeks and weeks, until in the summer of 1933, it emerged as the new silver-grey By-Pass. We were given a day off from school to watch its being officially opened by the Princess Royal. I did not see the Princess though, because Mum gave me a choice. She said, "Shall we go and see the Princess Royal? Or shall we use your day off to go and see Granma Farlow?"

Now Pankymoor, over the field near Wem, with my Granma and Grandad and Uncles and Aunties, was THE loveliest place on my earth, simply because they were there. I spent at least one week at Pankymoor every school holiday. I did not have to think twice. So - that was the day when the A5, the great London to Holyhead Road, changed its course, as a river might, on its way to Llangollen and North Wales, and when Shropshire's children sang songs for a Princess... and when Mum and I went in the sunshine to Wem, on a train from Upton Magna.

Joanie's other Granma, Granny Cockburn, and her aunties, lived in one of the smallholdings on the right hand side going up Emstrey Bank. We always looked out for them, to wave as we passed. All of the houses were identically plain, white and substantial. Each was set in a piece of land big enough for a small farm. Some had a poultry farm, some a few cattle, others a market garden. I had to count from the beginning to know for sure which was Joanie's Granny's, unless she happened to be in the garden.

Over on the skyline, beyond the fields on the opposite side of the road, a new row of shapes was growing every week. People pointed them out as "the new houses in Wenlock Road". From our distance in the bus they looked as though built of toy bricks.

A little later, if you looked up before you got too close, you saw Lord Hill on his Column. We looked in respectful amazement, and at his guarding lions as we passed. Another punctuation mark on our journey we saw from the English Bridge. We looked up and along the river to the solid towering Infirmary. Bright blobs, tiny against the greyness, Mum said, were beds outside on the open-air balcony. That was an era for Spartan faith in fresh-air healing.

Groans and straining of our loaded bus as it gained slowly up the steep Wyle Cop, was our signal to button up coats, fasten all purses, get a firm hold on the baskets, and be ready to leave the bus. Along the High Street past Della Porta's then turning, the bus crawled in front of the Shire Hall and joined its peers in The Square. A quick glance at the ancient clock told exactly how much time we had before the bus home.

The Market

We hurried down the steps and through the Gullet Passage. Things to be sold in the Market had to be attended to first. If there were a lot, Mum saw the man in charge and rented a yard or so of a long table-topped bench and the same distance of seat which ran behind it. If we only had a few things she might find somebody she knew and ask if they would mind trying to sell ours too, please. There were times when we got back from our shopping to find them still unsold.

Whichever way, a quick survey was first made to see, or rather to ask, the current price for whatever it was. Stallholders were strangely discreet about their prices. One had always to ask outright. Did the asking price vary, perhaps, according to who was asking?

Our own shopping involved joining a crowd of people at a stall where a pink-faced lady and her smaller bespectacled husband, both in white coats, were cheerily selling cheese. Large barrel shapes set into crusted greying muslin, like the ones in the cheese-room at Uckington, stood on the counter. More were stacked on the bench behind. Sliced through the middle into halves, they shone their moon faces of compacted pinky curd.

Mr and Mrs Burton came from Holloway Mouth, only a few yards from Moston, where I had been born at The Boat House. They knew both of my grandparent families well, and of course they had known me since before I was born. Mrs Burton gripped a wooden handle at the end of a wire, pulling it down through the cheese. The wire disappeared into a space between two wooden pieces of cheese-board. As half cheeses became wedges, then smaller wedges, and she handed us fragments to taste, she chatted family gossip.

She asked about my health. Did I like school? How old was I now? When were the school holidays? Would I be spending them with my Pankymoor Granma? She told of when she had last seen any of the family. Above all, every single time, it seemed, she said, "My word, what a big girl you are growing!"

Now, to be honest, I was sensitive about my size. But Mrs Burton was such a loving kind lady - and she was large, too - and I loved her as I loved my aunties, and

I knew she did not mean to hurt.

There were so many people and so many things in the Market. The sights and the smells of the cheeses and the chickens and gutted rabbits, of apples, raspberries, searching strawberries and purple damsons, of the mysteriously fragrant mint and sage, marjoram, lavender and mushrooms, the colour and the scent of primroses, cowslips, of spicy cottage pinks, sweet peas and chrysanthemums, all carried the seasons from Shropshire's country gardens into these solid Victorian walls. And then they carried them out again into the town's kitchens.

The sights and the smells were impressive, but what went deepest into me and has ever remained a part of me, was the feel of the sound of Shrewsbury Market. It was not a single sound, nor yet a number of sounds or conversations, but a babbling,continuous murmur like a forest in the wind. Some people hear a worldful of sound in a sea-shell. The setting for my sphere has been formed on a memory of harmonics which rose and fell and continued to chase and overlap each other, being caught and rebounding from high windows, then forever wandering softly within the sombre walls.

All the hundreds of voices, mellow voices of the border counties: "Lettuce - lovely rabbits - them beautiful beans! Cabbage? Ooo - ar, fresh cut this mornin' they wun, still got the dew on em! A nice chicken Missus? Them marras! rasberries... fresh butter... Surree they'm dear this wik! - a tuthree onions? What a pound are the damsons...?" Sometimes a sigh, "By eck, they inna wuth bringin in at this price!" and, "Ta-ta, then I'll tell yer a'nty I'n seen yer! HOW you are GROWIN!" All these and a million other snippets got themselves stirred into the acoustics to become the sound of the song of the spirit of the old Shrewsbury Market.

When there was a lot to sell, we might stay in town

for dinner and get a later bus. Of the two cafés among the smaller shops under the arch and beyond the butchers benches, in the outer arcade of the Market building, we chose Mrs. Machin's. They had tall narrow chairs, bench seats against the painted walls, and tables covered with light-patterned American oil-cloth. And the smell was distilled of tea-urn-tea, and Camp coffee and steam from boiling potatoes and reconstituted dried peas, of rich meaty sausages and warm sugary buns. There might have been other things on the menu, but I think not, for we always had exactly the same. Always, always potatoes were served plain boiled, never, never mashed or chips. It was not easy to control boiled potatoes and firm round peas, especially with an unfamiliar knife and fork. I used to feel I could have made better use of the gravy to combine them, had the potatoes only been mashed.

There were one or two assistants in overalls, but the dominant lady was dressed in Edwardian black. Her high crowned hat was trimmed round its narrow brim with bits of net and flowers. Her dress had a stand-up collar and shapely sleeves, and it almost reached to her booted ankles. Years later, in the early nineteen fifties, I took my own children in pushchairs to the same identical meal, with the same identical lady before the Market Hall was demolished and rebuilt.

In the corner of the old building, near the Mardol entrance, was Noblet's sweet shop. They sold an abundance of penny and ha'penny bargains, as well as packets of liquorice allsorts and fairy tale boxes of chocolates. Probably this was where Mrs Jebb at Beslow replenished her cave.

Another of the little shops sold sewing-machines. I cherished an ambition to own one somewhere in my distant future. Perhaps for my twenty-first birthday? That seemed a lifetime away - and a target at safe distance for the fulfilment of a dream.

Sometimes our first stop after the Market was a double-fronted shop at the top of Roushill Bank. I shall tell about Dad's bootmending another time, but Cranes' was where we bought the materials on a Saturday. I loved to go into that shop, with its rich smell of the leather stored in big flat sheets like table tops. Troughs of nails waited to be asked for by the pound weight and by length and thickness, and the shape of their heads. The dimness of the shop's light made grey lines on the face of the man who served us, making his face only a little lighter than his khaki overall and his lightish brown hair. He scooped the nails into the dish of one set of scales, and he weighed the cut squares of leather on a platform balance before packing them all into brown paper parcels.

If Dad needed a new shirt, or perhaps new neckbands for his old ones, or heavy thick silver-grey socks, we got these from Bradleys'. Tobacco we bought at Pelican Snelson's and I found my tongue sort of measuring out the name, Pe-li-can-Snel-son, Pe-li-can-Snel-son, almost like a sound you would find in a game rhyme – like Nebuchadnezzar!

Della Porta's stretched from High Street, behind the Shire Hall, right through to Princess Street. We often went there - for one thing, they had a very nice Ladies Room upstairs, with lavatories where there was a chain to pull when you'd finished, and paper which you tore off into tissue-paper squares - and mirrors for tidying your hair. For another thing, they sold things like embroidery and sewing-cotton. But what I liked most of all was that whatever we bought there was put into light brown paper-bags with chocolate-coloured spiders' webs drawn all over them. I've always had a passion for spiders' webs.

Whenever Mum went into Boots the Chemists, I had to wait outside. I suppose I would have asked "more questions than were good for you". Do you know, I grew up believing that children were not allowed in there? So I stood outside and I listened, and I learned the tune which the traffic sang up the steep Pride Hill.

The Bazaars and Places

Our expedition usually included the Bazaars. Woolworths labelled itself 'The 3d and 6d Stores'. Marks and Spencers, a bit up-market had a top price of five shillings - even for a party frock - supposing such item were on your list! At that time we did feel slightly apologetic about the bazaars. Whether the apology was to ourselves or to society, I cannot say. We had a kind of understanding that people who had plenty of money shopped elsewhere. Then, as Mum said, "Beggars can't be choosers!" We were certainly not beggars, though we had no choice but to buy where things were cheapest. The gleaming doorways of Maddox and Grocotts and perhaps most of the town-centre shops - except Della Porta's - were not for us. We glanced at their windows with 'new people' wearing fashionable clothes – and sometimes laughed at those fashions.

During the nineteen thirties, and for some years before and after, Shrewsbury's Woolworths was to the Market side of the Seventy Steps. Of course, between our Saturday buses we never had time to explore the steps.

At Woolworths, we bought gramophone needles in tiny tins, red, green or blue for loud, medium or soft, and sometimes a record. They sold smaller cheap recordings of popular songs with anonymous or less well-known singers. You could buy some for threepence. The real thing on ten-inch records cost a shilling and sixpence at Marks. A treat for me might be an Alice band with pretend diamonds on tortoiseshell, with elastic to hold it under my hair; Curly Top Shirley Temple was fashionable. I and most of the children I knew were plain, straight and unfashionable - but we tried. We used lots of slides and hairgrips with ornaments on them. Between the grips, we forced our stubborn straightness into exaggerated curves which we liked to think looked like waves.

Mum bought spectacles from Woolworths. She didn't want them all the time, she said, but for reading very small print; and she said they were making the eyes of needles smaller nowadays. It was the only pair she had until after the National Health Service began, more than ten years later.

Woolworths held two favourite spots for me. First was the Refreshment Bar in the basement. When time and money could be spared, this was a special treat. We only rarely had coffee at home, and I sought it as a luxury whenever I could. The smell of it met me halfway down Woolworths stairs, and drew me to its source. I always chose the same: milky coffee, and creamy shreds of cheese pressed with sliced tomatoes into square sandwiches. We always had round cottage loaves at home.

It was not only the food there which excited me, though. I was fascinated by the row of brightly-coloured bottles along the front of the glass case. They stood roughly level with my eyes and I read their labels as I munched. Lemon and orange I had met before, but cherryade, ginger beer, ice-cream soda and vivid green lime were new to me. There was even something I used to read to be claret, until I learned that claret was something quite different. But strangest of all, 'Dan-de-lion and Bur-dock' it said. What in the world...? Was that really something you could drink? The brown fluid itself held something of a threat, reminding me of Mum's home-made Wormwood Tea. Someone had told her that wormwood tea would be good for my impetigo which plagued me every summer. I had hard memories of being chased round the kitchen where we lived at Marton, by Mum with wormwood tea in her one hand and a ginger biscuit in the other to take the taste away - if I was good and drank the medicine. Poor Mum had had to give up that remedy. But Dan-de-lion and Bur-dock...? Hmm... It looked - and it sounded - suspicious. I never did taste the bright drinks, my eyes played games with their jewel colours whilst I smelt and drank the glorious coffee.

I had a distant aunty and uncle who lived in Shrewsbury. Their son and his young lady had been in a motorbike accident at Yorton one bank holiday. The young man had been killed, but the lady, recovered from injuries, was back at her job, in Woolworths. It was characteristic of Mum's nature that she insisted on catching the eye of the right fair-haired young lady in her dark red uniform, and smiling and waving a greeting. This done, we left by the back stairs.

This brought me to another of my favourite bits of the bazaars. To be honest I am not certain whether it was in Woolworths or in Marks and Spencers, that the back staircase had a window about half-way up (or down). I liked to stand there as long as Mum would let me. For, far away down below the roof-tops were the empty pens of the cattle-market. Empty, that is, except for one Saturday a month, when the horse auction was (the cattle auction was held every Tuesday). There was something sad about all the lovely horses, all shapes and colours and ages, standing and waiting, for their fate to be decided for them by small huddles of farming folk - and by the nodding and shaking of heads. Beyond the Smithfield Road ran the river, then fields and foundries, churches and all kinds of buildings and roof-tops, as the town rolled steeply upwards again towards Wales.

Further along the street, beyond the bazaars, was Melias, the grocers. Waiting for our turn always seemed endless. Eventually we were next. A large sheet of brown paper was laid on the counter. As Mum read each item on her list, the assistant fetched it, laying each one carefully to the centre of the paper. When everything was together and Mum paid the bill, the back and front edges of the paper were lifted together, folded and pleated into a firm enclosing strip. Then the side ends were shaped and crisply creased, and the whole parcel tailored exactly as needed to carry our particular groceries. Tough string went twice round each both ways, hooked through where it crossed itself in the middle, underneath and on top, firmly tied with quick fingers, then - SNAP! I was never sure whether it was a cutter, or a practised sleight of hand which parted the string. But to watch the deft movements by which our parcel came together was worth all the waiting. Our name was written on the folded top –

"Which buz is it, Mrs Farlow?"

"The twelve o'clock please. You will see that it gets there, won't you?"

They always did... except once. Then Mum had to walk all the six miles home, much of the way without a footpath along the busy London road, carrying the parcel and the other shopping. I was not with her that day. I had got Dad an improvised dinner, and he was back at work when she staggered in.

"Oh dear," she flopped. "I'm about jiggered up. The parcel hadn't come. The blimmin' buz wouldn't wait. It would have to happen the first day into town after that blessed old flu!"

From Melias we always hurried to the butchers. At that time we were getting our meat from Davies's at the top of the Cop, just past the pillar-box and the steps to the church. Dad knew what he liked when it came to meat - and it had to be beef –

"A nice piece of beef, please, not more than half a crown," was our regular request. I had to memorise it for when I went alone. The butcher, who I always took to be Mr Davies, was cheerful. He had straight black hair and thick eyebrows. His eyes twinkled as if she had bought half the shop, or at least half an animal instead of half a crown's worth. Joint chosen, price agreed and joint wrapped, he pressed the change enthusiastically into her hand, always with the same cheerful voice and the same expression –

"Chablarged!" I could not make it out.

"Thankyou, Goodbye," said Mum.

"Good mornin', Mrs Farlow. Chablarged!" said he.

In time I gave up trying to work out what he said, and asked Mum straight out what he meant.

"He's simply thanking us for shopping there," she explained. "He says he is 'much obliged' to us for our custom. We might have bought our meat in the market."

"Oh," I thought, "Chablarged" means "Chabliged" which means, "I am much obliged to you for buying your meat here." Oh, I see... "Chablarged..."

Back at the Square, we first sought the Melias' boy with the parcel, then joined familiar faces among those waiting along the pavement near the Old Plough and Grocott's window, glad if there were a few minutes in hand by the Square's clock.

A number of buses were standing, loading or unloading. As each one left, it was replaced by another. The uniformed inspector was in control of it all. From his bright outdoor face under the peaked cap, the music of Shropshire place-names trumpeted forth. A soft Salopian voice does not naturally carry over the noise of revving engines. The vowel sounds need to be sharpened for the job. The places where all these people lived became known to me simply by the pictures my mind drew as he called the names:

"PLOX GREEN – MinsterLAY."

"EBButs Rerwd !"

"CHARCH Strett'n - LudLERW!"

"RUYT'n LEYven TERWNS!"

"DITTon PRARRS!" ... and so on.

Soon it was "ETCHem n WELLin TON!" and we climbed on –"Will you stop at the lane end past *The Horse Shoe,* please?"

Chapter Ten

The Big Room at Donnington

Writing Lessons

Once upon a time there had been three teachers at Donnington School. The Mistress taught the Infants, the Master taught the oldest third or so, and a younger lady had taught the middle ones in the first half of the Big Room. That lady left round about the time I moved up from the Infants, and she was not replaced. So everyone from around seven years to fourteen was under the direct charge of the Master.

We sat in pairs at double desks, according to age, about six, or perhaps eight, in each 'standard'. Under each desk top was a shelf, with a canvas bag, which had been sewn by the girls to hold books, rulers and pens and such-like. For an occasional Spring Clean the bags were allotted to the girls, to be taken home and washed. The Mistress told us how, during our sewing lessons.

"In order to remove ALL the grime and stains, you must first soak the bag overnight in COLD WATER. You must NOT plunge the article into HOT water. That will only serve to harden in the stains. Now, HOW do you set about getting the dirt out?"

"Soak the bag in cold water, um," the chorus recited.

"Very well! The following day you may use hot water - as hot as you can bear it, with your soap-powder. Do you all understand?"

"Yes, um."

"There will be a pot of jam, tell your mothers, for the girl who brings back the cleanest bag."

Mum had some washing-powder called *Glee.* I

suppose it must have been good because then I was the bearer-home of a jar of plum jam.

There must have been planning in a syllabus to cover and interleave the needs of our differing ages and abilities, and yet to us it did not show. To us, it seemed we had a lesson in this or that subject entirely at the Master's whim. Nothing was predictable – to us. It sometimes happened we learned the same lesson more than once, or perhaps it was that we overheard and took note of other people's instruction whilst supposedly getting on with our own.

Certainly the same titles for homework compositions cropped up frequently, particularly the practical ones: 'How to Clean a Pair of Shoes', 'How to light a Fire', and 'A Description of My School', came round so often we almost knew our own words by heart.

We wrote that, "The school was built in 1874 to serve the parishes of Wroxeter and Uppington. It was, therefore, situated at Donnington, which is equi-distant between the two villages. The name of the school is 'Wroxeter and Uppington School...' and so on." We knew the measurements of each of the rooms, the height of the windows and other statistics which, mercifully, I have forgotten. There was, in fact a history of education earlier at Donnington.

Once, for home-work, we were asked to describe a picture - any picture which we had at home –

"Tell me what it looks like, who painted it, and why you like it - and anything at all you can tell about it," the Master said.

We had a picture which I had lived with and through a lot in my few years. I had watched it and thought about the people in it in bright daylight, at dusk in the flickering firelight, and in the lamplight's shadows. So I wrote about it - a man wearing a kilt, a bit like mine, his knees bare over his socks like my winter ones. He had one arm in a sling. His head rested on the shoulder of a lady with a blue madonna scarf round her head, and a large baby on her arm. Buttercups were strewn on the floor near the lady's bare feet; there was a dog with a collie-tail, like Izzie at the farm, and an old-fashioned soldier with a bunch of keys. The name of the picture was *'The Order For Release'*. On and on I wrote. There was several inches of small print under the picture which told me all about it and the man who painted it.

The Master was impressed, and for a time it seemed my family's standing went up in his eyes. He questioned Mum when she came to school on Dentist Day.

"I understand you have an interesting picture at your house, Mrs Farlow."

"Have we?" Mum was puzzled. I don't think she had remembered about the writing. "Oh, yes? And what picture would that be?"

She was surprised when he told her. She had saved the page from a calendar. She'd framed it in brown imitation wood because she liked it, and because, as was her way, she felt something for the people in it - not at all because she thought it was important. I think the Master was relieved that it was not a 'proper' painting as he understood them, and my family could resume its natural level in society.

I had a hard job to please the Master in many things, but usually I managed it with writing, especially home-work compositions, when I could take as long as I needed. He always read aloud the story from his *Teachers'* magazine for us to remember and tell in our words. He handed us each a single sheet of lined paper.

"If you need more paper, or if you lose this one, use any paper you can find. Do the whole composition on SUGAR-paper if you like, so long as you DO it. I will accept NO excuse!" What was sugar-paper?

Once he rewarded me with two pennies, praise indeed from him to me, for a 'Teacher' story, about a dog who waited all night outside a shop-door because his master had left by another and forgotten him.

Once Cadbury's promoted a competition for an account of the growth and manufacture of their cocoa and chocolate. Our imagination ran riot as the Master read the list of prizes. The first was a Treasure Chest full of bars of chocolate and boxes of chocolates and chocolate creations we had never heard of. He did say that IF our school won First Prize, or any other, the writer or writers would not enjoy the bounty to themselves, but would share it with the school.

A new word entered our vocabulary as we began to study the chocolate story: 'Cacao' beans grow on cacao trees in the Gold Coast, which was in Africa.

"They used to call it *'The White Man's Grave'*," the Master reminisced. Firms such as Cadburys changed the cacao beans into cocoa and into chocolate. I soon knew the story by heart and enjoyed getting all the details of the manufacturing process on to paper.

I was thrilled to be among the winners and Donnington School won the First Prize. Each of the writers received a bar to take home and everyone had a chocolate nibble of some kind. There were a few murmurings that the writers should have had more for themselves, but it didn't seem ever so important. That the actual chocolate seemed rather ordinary compared with the big build-up perhaps served in itself to illustrate certain differences between expectations and realisation. Yet it was nice that my essay won a prize.

Practice in writing of a less creative, if more socially useful kind, came round frequently. Half pages of tiniest squared paper were distributed. Inkwells filled, nibs renewed. The Master wrote the pattern on the board. In our very, very best printed writing we headed the notice. *'Wroxeter and Uppington Cricket Club'* - or sometimes it was some other organisation. We spaced out carefully over the tiny squares that a meeting - or a Whist Drive – or a Rummage Sale - or perhaps a Dance - would be held at the Parish Room Wroxeter, or the Duke Room Uppington on such a day and at such a time, and so on. The work was performed very reverently, with bated breath for NO mistakes were permitted. The notices were folded and tucked in and addressed. The joy of this project, for we Uckington Ones, was that there would invariably be one to be delivered to the Crows' house at Beslow on our way home. We could have popped it through the door, of course, but we always knocked and waited to be smiled at as we handed it directly into the actual hands of the Gorgeous Mrs Crow herself!

Rods and music

On the whole I enjoyed lessons. On the whole I did well - but there were exceptions. The twin banes of my school work were related: pen-nibs and inkwells. Pen-nibs were forever getting themselves crossed, making my letters and figures all straggly and scratchy; tiny china inkwells forever running dry, or, more rarely, over-full. I was too cowardly to politely point out defects in our equipment. It took enormous effort to scrape the last film of blue-black dried out at the bottom of the miniature pot. First by licking the nib, then by persistently mixing it with spit, the sediment was reconstituted into the last shadow of colour. Had the pot itself been other than white, I swear I would have used that colour too. Eventually the wretched thing was refilled. Then, inevitably, with misused pen-nib I got blots all over the place – and over me. It was a rare and delightful luxury when ink and paper and pen were such that I could produce an acceptable page of writing. Meanwhile I suffered the Master's knuckles round my forehead for my untidy work.

"What do you call this?" he roared. "Looks like flies round a jampot! - or a spider who's walked through it!"- the knuckles again - "Slovenly Selina! - that's what we'll call YOU!"

Perhaps he was right, for my life has been one long and losing struggle for tidiness. Once, too, I got into trouble with the Master for daring to use joined handwriting! That was quite forbidden - we were required to print.

I suppose I muttered objections from my desk for from time to time I was called out to receive the cane. "Insubordination" was the word the master used. It followed that nobody liked to be caned, but not everybody wept about it. I honestly think I could have borne the sting on my hand, if only those stupid scalding tears had not insisted on humiliating me. However hard I tried, they always did.

There were occasions when some of the boys had a beating. Then the Master's anger, his arm raised before bringing down the cane over the boy with the yellow hair, the boy's red face, humiliation and the hurt in his eyes and his yelling, turned my limbs to jelly as the rest of us tried to keep our heads bowed, and concentrate on our lessons.

Library days were nice days - and they at least were regular. There was a grown-ups' book-box as well as our own, and we took books home for our parents. The wooden boxes arrived from the County Library, and each book had the Salop County Council mark embossed in a circle on its cover. I liked to rub my pencil over a piece of thin paper and copy the circle patterns. Especially I loved the smell of the library books. For myself, I always chose stories about boarding schools.

Of our erratic time-table, perhaps our most erratic lesson of all was music. There were odd moments when we learned that Every Good Boy Deserves a Fiddle, and that spaces spell F A C E . We learnt about the length of the musical notes, but I would have dearly liked to have learnt more about music, to have understood about keys and things. Our singing was related to seasons and to special events. Each year we sang:

> *"Dressed in brightest yellow see*
> *The daffodils gleam fair*
> *Under the cold March skies.*
> *Let us ask them lovingly*
> *Why, when the fields are bare,*
> *They open wide their eyes."*

From all childhood's songs it is that simple one which stays most in my mind. We learnt *'Land of our Birth'* and other patriotic hymns and songs, for the Princess Royal's Empire Day, and for the Silver Jubilee, and for the Coronation which did not happen – and again for the one which did.

Everybody was excited at the coming of the school wireless. We talked a lot about the wonder of it.

"How many of you have a wireless set at home?" the Master asked. A sprinkling of hands went up.

"Harold, have you ever looked at the back of your wireless set?"

"Yes, Sir." Harold was taken by surprise.

"What did you see?"

"Wires, Sir."

"Then why it is that we call it a 'wireless', eh? How do you account for that?"

In my memory, Harold always wore dark blue, either a suit or a knitted jersey with coloured bands. He had a fresh country colour to his cheeks, brown eyes and black hair.

Flustered a little, his pink face reddened: "I - I dunno, Sir." There followed a lesson on some of the principles of radio, and telephone systems. Lessons seemed to come to us like that, spontaneously - and knowledge to reach us almost incidentally. We never knew what was coming next.

The wireless arrived at school exactly in time for us

to listen to the launching ceremony of a great new ship. The Queen was to perform the launching and to name the ship. We were asked to consider likely names for a luxury liner. The Master brought his *Daily Sketch* with pictures and descriptions of it. There were ballrooms and shops and cinemas and all sorts of things, which made it seem more like a city than a ship.

Apart from Nelson's *'Victory'*, the only ship name I knew was *'The Revenge'* from a poem. The Master often read to us dramatically that -

"At Flores, in the Azores, Sir Richard Grenville lay..."

- and about the brave little ship *'Revenge'*. Neither name seemed appropriate for a luxury liner, though. Our imagination did not run to the Queen naming it after herself.

The first Royal voice we had ever heard spoke out from the box on the wall of our school room –

"I name this ship *'The Queen Mary'*...."

The event stayed in our minds, not only because of the newness of the wireless and the greatness of the occasion. It was made the more potent for us by the picture which also hung on the same wall. This was of King George V and Queen Mary in their youth. He stood and she sat looking into our schoolroom with all their Royal dignity. Her hair was piled high and fixed with jewels, and there were more jewels about her neck, her arms and over her bodice and a silk sash shone draped diagonally over her front. He looked a symbol of powerfulness, with a heavy moustache. Gold buttons and ribbons and medals lit up his dark uniform jacket.

If we had expected that the coming of the school wireless would bring regularity to our lesson pattern, we were mistaken. For that was one of only three broadcasts I remember hearing during the years that the wireless and I shared the schoolroom. Another was the launching, sometime later, of an even bigger liner, the *Queen Elizabeth*. This time we were prepared for the name and it was not so exciting.

The other broadcast was of singing by a choir of school-children from Manchester. The sound of their voices was unbelievable - and as different from our own ragged music-making as is a nightingale from a farmyard chicken. Could that music really be made by children like us? Well, perhaps not quite like us. Yet, even our singing was sometimes asked for. A few times the Master rehearsed us well to take part as a choir at special services at Wroxeter Church, such as when somebody important got married and asked that the children should sing, please. Then we sang about –

> *"The Voice that breath'd o'er Eden,*
> *that earliest wedding day," and a Psalm about -*
> *"Lifting eyes unto the hills,*
> *from whence cometh my help."*

We understood about looking at hills.

And on that same long wall as the King and Queen and the new school wireless was the clock.

At our table

Its large white face hung on the back wall opposite the fireplace. Its bland expression, through its Roman numbers, gazed indifferently over our backs. Its pendulum impassively tapped away all those minutes which seemed like hours and the years which now seem to have gone in as many minutes.

When the morning seemed to have lasted forever, the Master announced the time.

"Stand by your desks! Hands together – eyes closed." Inky fingers came stickily together. A deep breath, as it were to get us in step: "One. Two!"

Be pre-sent at our ta-ble Lord –(breath)

Be here and ev-ry where ad-ored – (breath)
Thy crea tures bless and grant that we – (breathe)
May feast in Pa-ra-dise with Thee.

A- A- A- A- M E E E N !"

Lead away quietly!

As quietly and as orderly as hollow stomachs would let us, we filed into the cloakrooms. The Donnington Ones quickly grabbed coats and vanished. The rest of us groped into the accumulated smells of daily sandwiches for crumpled paper parcels and glass bottles from our schoolbags.

As a general rule, our 'table' was likely to be a lean-up against the iron railings, or against a patch of school wall. In hot summer we were allowed to sit on the grass of the orchard between the playground and the school house. If rain came we tramped to cover through channels of dust on the floor of the open fronted 'shed'. Discarded wooden desks with long bench seats had been left here for our playtime use. We could make floppy 'castles' of the dry dust, or plough shapes in it with our feet. Then the pattern of our sandals was reversed onto socks, and we knew we would be called to account for the mess.

"Ooh - just look at your socks, our Mary! Our Mum wun'arf go on at you!"

"I can'elp it if the ground's all dusty. We canna stay out there in the wet!"

An enamel bowl and carbolic soap stood by the rainwater tub for our handwashing. At the opposite corner, beyond the shed, was the row of what grownups insisted on calling WCs. As each day progressed, the buckets became worryingly full and contributed, I suspect, to the occasional mishap, and to many more nightmares.

Any settled-in heat wave-brought a short craze for picnicks in the field next to the school. Then some of the children played at 'Marathons', running all the way round the field, close to the hedges. It was a big field, the one the

Uppington Ones already crossed twice daily by a path through the middle. It was all the rest of us could do to distinguish which runner was who when they reached the far hedge. Lazy ones cheered home the wet and red faces. I hated running! I was one who stayed to make daisy-chains and look for four-leaf clovers.

Some playground games I enjoyed: hopscotch, skipping, ball games, especially two-ball. Many games involved a rhyme of some kind to record competitive progress, like –
"NEB-ud-cadNEZ-ar the KING of the JEWS -
BOUGHT his WIFE a PAIR of SHOES!" -and
"SILK, SATin, MUSlin, RAGS!" - or
"SALT, MUSTard, VIN-egar, CAY- enne PEP- per!"
I quite thought cayenne was something other than pepper.

I would have given the earth to have been able to do handstands. Try as I would, I seemed to have been wrongly constructed. All I managed was grazed knees, hands imprinted with gravelly ground, and a great deal of humiliation - so I gave up.

All we girls enjoyed ring games, and how those songs stay in the mind! –
"The farmer's in his den, the farmer's in his den –
Ee I diddely I - the farmer's in his den!"
And -
"The wind, the wind, the wind blows high,
The rain comes scattering down the sky,
He is handsome, she is pretty:
She is the girl of the London City.
She goes courting one- two- three:
Pray and tell me who is he..."
(whisper, whisper,...) and so on.

Oh, but that intrusive London City! Such a symbol of perfection was it held to be, that it seemed that everything which might be wrong with our lives was wrong, simply because where we were was not London. For to us it was THE CITY of kings and queens and fairy-tales, of government and power, of jubilees and coronations and Royal weddings in golden coaches, all drawn along by prancing white horses. Scenes we saw in the papers merged in our imagination with Cinderella and Dick Whittington. Seat of all history and source of all magic, it fused in our minds and overlapped with the Biblical City of Gold!

Great though London undoubtedly was when eventually some of us met it face to face we had a measure of disappointment. For its buildings were not of crystal or gold, but common bricks and mortar or stone, set on to solid earth, much as Shrewsbury's were, only more so. Its people wore coats and hats and shoes, if newer than ours, no wispy tulle or coronets. The trains which bore us to London were the same that took us away from Shrewsbury - no transformation as we came nearer to the magic. Even the buses were red, not <u>so</u> different from our 'Midlands', not a whimsical chariot - nor a golden coach to be seen. Exciting though the immensity and the bustle of London was, it lacked something of the glory of its reputation. Yet throughout our playground games and our drawings of what we thought London was like, we had not yet shed our illusions.

In the worst winter weather we could spend dinner times in our classrooms. Standing round the heavy mesh fireguards, we played guessing or pencil-and-paper games. We laughed ourselves into stitches at our unlikely 'consequences', and we were obsessed with list-and-letter games. And, of course, we could get on with our knitting or sewing.

Most memories of dinner-times are memories of games, for the time spent eating was short. We were ravenous for those paste or jam 'pieces', and they were quickly gone.

Drink was usually lemonade from powder or crystals. Thermos flasks were too fragile and too expensive for us. Tea, when we took that, was in a glass bottle wrapped in several thicknesses of newspaper. If not hot, it was perhaps not quite cold by the time we drank it. The milky sweet smell of tea-sodden cork seemed an extension of the liquid. Together they were unique, and the drink not altogether unpleasant - if you could forget it was tea.

For a time in the coldest depth of winter, we were encouraged to take a cup from home, with a spoonful each of cocoa and sugar, and enough milk to persuade the stubborn, floaty powder into a paste. Flapper Parry was one of the big girls. She was in charge of boiling the big black kettle on the open fire of the Big Room, then she poured the scalding hot water into our cups. Remembering now makes me panic, yet I don't remember anyone coming to grief that way. I think we must have been a fairly responsible crowd of children, at least some of the time. Perhaps conditions bred us to cope with them. Perhaps we were what was known as being 'old for our years'.

Flapper, whose real name was Betty, was popular at dinner-times on another count. Her mother kept a small shop, selling sweets and tobacco, at Norton. (This was a second shop at Norton). Flapper kept a list of sweet orders to bring next day, cash either with order, or on delivery. And Flapper sang us songs from 'Top Hat', and some other films.

One of my happiest Donnington memories is of the first ever school milk. It was not only that milk at school was unfamiliar: many of us had never seen milk in bottles. (At Uckington, we waited in the farm dairy whilst the milk flowed in waves down a silver-coloured cooler which looked like a washboard. Into a channel it went, then through a hole, whence it was caught on its way to the churn. I liked to wait and watch the dance of the wavy milk as it stilled into our enamel can.)

Now this other milk came to school - in third of a pint bottles. (I expect that was the day some of us began to learn fractions.) They chinked and gleamed - like snowdrops growing in metal crates. Row upon row of them stood, each with a cream line teasing an inch or so down from the tops. Round cardboard tops had the farmer's name, and he became important to us. If we pressed the tiny centre disc too hard we got cream on our fingers - or worse, it squirted to tragic waste. I have never enjoyed a drink as much - ever - as that cool milk taste, through the real straw the golden colour and texture of harvest fields. Too soon contented gulps gave way to hollow spluttering as we chased the last film of it in the angle of the bottle. It cost a ha'penny a bottle, tuppence ha'penny a week, but if mothers could manage fivepence, we could have one at dinner time as well as playtime.

On frosty mornings the crate was placed near the fire. This did no more than warm the bottles nearest the heat. The milk was hardly at all less cold. But warmish or cold, colder or coldest, it was truly delicious.

Questions, questions

If music at Donnington was seasonal and erratic, dramatic art was almost non-existent. Once in my earliest Donnington years, there was a concert in the school. We walked with our parents on a dark winter's evening. The Big Room was transformed, the end nearest the Infants Room lit up for a stage. We were part of the audience who peered from the darkness of the other end. There was dressing-up and jokes and singing and a lot of laughing. Eddie Brayley was one of the big boys. He sang about "Following in Father's Footsteps". His father kept a bicycle-shop in Shrewsbury. It was a joyful night, mysterious and magical - but for whatever reason, it never happened again.

It was on a brilliant summer's day that we took part, with other schools, in a missionary event. It was held in another school or perhaps a village hall, probably

Leighton. Each school was required to present a sketch illustrating the work of missionaries in a different country. Our country was India. We each wore a sari in a lovely colour. Mine was a sort of light bluey-green. We were to stand gracefully, whilst certain of us told the story, more or less in mime, with very little speaking. Perhaps the technique was too sophisticated, both for audience and players, for our sketch was less well received than the others. Certainly I had no idea what it meant, and I got into trouble with the Master for standing almost behind the curtain.

"Why do you have to stand where you can't be seen, Farlow?" he demanded, with one of his characteristic hard-knuckle nudges. I expect he felt let down at our not having brought credit to the school. Nothing like that event ever happened again either, but I remember the stage and the other children and the sunshine - and we Donnington ones in saris - and being surprised that the saris stayed on, their seemingly being simply folded into place.

As well as Christmas and Easter, two annual happenings contributed to our 'Scripture' lessons. The Scripture Examination was held every June. The vicar, Rev. Hobbs from Wroxeter, came to school first thing in the morning. One by one he tested our biblical knowledge. Those who answered enough questions correctly were given a certificate signed by himself and by the Bishop of Lichfield. Then we all went home - in the middle of the morning! And always that was a hot bursting with sunshine June morning. One of those sweetest essence-of-summer memories is of my walking along the path between the Luthers' Canterbury bells, with bees buzzing into the hot spiciness of pinks and Sweet Williams - at the unfamiliar home-time of just before noon, the hens cackling their own tune through the brilliance, and me carrying my new certificate to show Mum.

Our other annual religious learning was The

Catechism. Every year some children were of an age to be confirmed and every year, it seemed, we all learned the procedure by rote.

"What is your name?"

"N or M."

"Who gave you this name?"

"My Godfathers and my Godmothers in my Baptism..."

In unison we recited the whole, questions and answers, the "I believe", the Ten Commandments, as well as the Lord's Prayer. Our tongues were trained around Sacraments and Sureties, around repentance and righteousness. We practiced the Order for Confirmation, singing our own liturgical responses to the Master's intoning of the Bishop's parts.

Now I must not - indeed I cannot - draw conclusions as to the effect of that learning on the future Christian lives of most of us there. But, for reasons best known to Himself, God had made me with just a streak of a rebel, with a ready tendency to question established routine. The learning by rote of Christian principles meant less to me, personally, than the times-tables which we similarly chanted. For me such mystical statements required other expression than the mechanics of arithmetic. The seeds of the first flutterings of my own spiritual enlightening reached me scattered from other directions, though heaven knows they took time to mature. Their scattering provided me with a dimension for comparison with school's religious training.

In the first place, both Mum and Dad had been brought up 'chapel'. At one time Mum had used to walk all the way from Welshampton to Wem Methodists, and that was where they had been married. It was the Methodist Minister who had christened me, at home when I was six weeks old because I had chicken-pox. Mum sang chapel hymns around the house, like "Jesus, Friend of little children", and I puzzled a lot about one of the lines.

"Shew me what my love should cherish" was all right, but then she sang "Wotuitshdshun" - yes, truly, "Wotuitshdshun"! It was not until spelling and punctuation were learned that "What, too, it should shun" was revealed and another problem solved. Even so, I listened in vain for Mum's hymns at school.

In the second place, when I spent school holidays with Granma Farlow, at Pankymoor, just outside Wem, Sundays meant walking to chapel morning and evening, over the field, along the road, under the railway bridge, and past the mill, our feet keeping time to the church bells. We cut through the churchyard, under the pealing bells, down the little street by the grocer's to the Baptist Chapel. In the afternoon we did it again, with Auntie Alice. She taught at the Sunday School; she led me through a solid wooden doorway, under an arch and down some steps into the large semi-basement room. A lady named Eileen played the piano, and a boy named Les played a violin, and we all sang from bendy Golden Bells hymnbooks with green cloth covers. And we sang about -

"Beautiful words, wonderful words,
Wonderful words of life!" -

and we sang about throwing out a lifeline across the dark wave, that there was a brother whom someone should save! Perhaps it was because of Ginny Greenteeth threatening from her water in the pits and the Front Field well, that a hymn about a lifeline struck home with me.

And from yet a third direction... Back at Uckington Joan and Barbara and George's Grandad Evans was a preacher. Most Sunday mornings he invited me to go with them in the big plum and black Wolseley motor car. It might be to Rodington or Marsh Green chapels, if he was preaching or had someone to see there, otherwise it was to Tan Bank Methodist Church in Wellington. We were not so fond of Tan Bank: it was big and formal, and the preacher was high up and remote. They sang "O Worship the King" nearly every Sunday. They sang it so often that we naughty Uckington children more or less had bets on it. Then we got the giggles. It was a wonder we were still taken.

But the village chapels were little bigger than a cottage sitting-room. They had dado borders painted round their middles, where the colours met, and there were verses lettered out over the pulpit. And here the preachers - sometimes it was Joan's Grandad, sometimes Mr Birch who brought our bread to Uckington and who was so kind about the bill - whoever it was the preacher preached with passion and sometimes with tear-light in his eyes. And here we sang about children being wanted by Jesus - to be 'jewels' in His crown, and for 'sunbeams to shine for Him', and to be 'like a little candle burning in the night'. I had a special feeling for candlesticks, not formal ecclesiastical candlesticks, but the flat, 'Wee Willie Winkie' type with a little round handle for your fingers. Mum always preferred tiny oil lamps, but I had a yearning for a candlestick. As for me being wanted – like a candle - well... Think of it - ME! Oh, dear, though, I could be so very naughty. Something of the enthusiasm and the atmosphere, of the pictures and the poetry, made its impression on me. Our catechism exercise at Donnington was well intentioned of course but... well, I suppose it lacked the tear-light, somehow.

The people at Rodington and Marsh Green let us Uckington girls take part in their Sunday School Anniversary. We could sit with their children at the front and sing special hymns and say recitations. Aunty Alice from Pankymoor always made me a new dress for the event, and we all wore straw-hats with wide brims and tiny flowers on them. Then we stayed for tea and the Evening Service, and we went for walks in their fields and along the river bank, or perhaps it was a canal? It was along that water's edge that I first saw dragonflies lit up in the mid-summer sunshine and darting over the water, and there that yellow flag irises first became my favourite flowers.

And that was where I fell in love - with shimmering silver-blue dragonflies - and with a boy named Arthur, who was eleven and almost grown up.

Spring into summertime

Perhaps it was because our light came only from the day or dimly from oil lamps, and our warmth, only from the sun or the kitchen fire, that the seasons' boundaries seem to have been more sharply defined in our tiny hamlet community in the nineteen thirties. Was Uckington even a hamlet? - having not more than a dozen houses, including the farm and the pub? It was certainly not a village. Mum said that a proper village a place had to have a church, and even a school. We had three churches to choose from, but none of them less than two miles away.

As days began to lengthen, Dad, though always busy, applied extra bustle in the direction of the garden. The powers which organised our lives must have agreed with him, when 'they' said that the clocks must be pushed forward to give an 'extra hour' of precious daylight around tea-time. Then Dad went straight into the garden from work before having his tea, to make the most use of daylight. Last year's carrots were coming to their end, and what remained of the apples were yellow and wrinkling and felt sort of spongy. The earth seemed to be stirring from its rest and turning its face towards summer again.

Days and weeks - and the years - seemed longer then. At around five to ten or so years old, we knew there was a lot for us to learn all the time. At the earliest beginnings of summer we somehow expected to have become quite different people by the end of it. Life, like the seasons, was all expectation.

As days began to warm we no longer wanted to

hurry over the fields and along the lanes to, and especially from school. The lanes and the cart-tracks became places to be, places in their own right, not merely to be passed through. They shewed us some of their secrets at that quickening time before they got themselves covered with greenery.

Trailing our coats, still in our winter clothes we dawdled our way home peering at a world coming to life. We watched the progress of nest building and noted which birds lined them with mud. We rejoiced at their first eggs and counted the days until the young birds would hatch. We were even allowed to take an occasional egg, provided it was not more than one from a nest and that we did not touch the others. We learnt the delicate art of blowing the contents from the fragile blue shell. If hatching took longer than expected, we felt gently with the backs of fingers. Cold shells meant the parents had deserted, either frightened away or killed.

The daffodil songs we sang at school gave way to cuckoo songs and the cuckoo himself called over our way as regularly as April came. Raucous noises screeched through blades of hard grass as we blew into them pressed between our thumbs. The lanes became banked with cow parsley as high as ourselves, and powdery lace flowers ticked our faces when we stood amongst them.

Some days we walked home with the Uppington ones, over all their fields. Then we crossed a short stretch of old Roman road where we collected tufts of wool left on the hedges by the sheep - and we considered all the stages before it could be knitted. It's funny how you remember things: it was on one of those journeys, as we were near Uppington Church, that Connie Pritchard shewed me a new copper threepenny bit, with six sides, like the holes in a honeycomb. They were to replace our silver ones.

It was dawdling home in the between seasons of winter clothes and summer sunshine that I particularly remember us pondering and practising some of our newly learnt vocabulary: some of it wholesome - some less so. I don't mean swearing, of course. Though we knew about that, it was quite forbidden in Uckington households. Even the menfolk used swear words only in anger or extreme frustration, never as a matter of course, like some other families did. No, I'm telling about some of the more subtle components of our Shropshire conversation.

Some words were part of our vocabulary simply because we were where we were. Words like 'brivit', and 'gleedy' and 'tranklements' and 'tuthree' were used quite innocently, not knowing that elsewhere in England they might be meaningless. We also became aware of certain other differences between the language spoken around us and that which education was revealing in our lessons. The word 'chimney', for instance. Some of us had greatest difficulty spelling it. For surely 'chimbley' had to be spelt with a 'b' in the middle - didn't it? Then as we got on to plurals, some people were used to speaking about birds 'nesses' and winter 'vesses', not to mention 'crusses' on the bread. Everyone knew what was meant of course, but our Uckington mothers said that was a rough way to speak, and we had not to speak like that. There were yet other features of our Shropshire inheritance, used regularly by our menfolk, but discouraged among 'respectable', if working-class, women and children. So we had to practice such unladylike expressions as 'summat' and 'nowt', in private so to speak, with such as these we indulged ourselves on our dawdly way home.

To the birds and the budding honeysuckle, and to the bees among the dogroses we chanted:
"Yer munna say wunna - it inner polite,
An yer conna say shonna - 'cos that binna right!"

Photos and summer food

Whenever my aunties came to visit us, they brought a camera. They had taken photos of me from when I was tiny. But whilst I was six, Mum decided I should have my photograph taken - in a shop! I had to dress up in my newest frock. Aunty Alice from Pankymoor made me one every year. This particular one was mauve, the bodice made of voile, which you could see through in between the white pansies over it. The skirt was plain cotton, the colour of pale violets. Mr Beedles, Joanie's Dad, had cut my hair into a fringe style. (Mum always paid him with a packet of Players for cutting all our hair.) We brushed and combed mine until it shone round my podgy face.

The photo-shop was 'Stanleys' Studios' in Shrewsbury, at the top of The Cop, near to Davies's our butcher's. The room up the steps was gloomy and mysterious with aspidistra plants and a lot of dark polished wood. They set me to stand by a low table, with a light shining on me. I had to place my hands on an open magazine and pretend to be interested in the pictures. Then the man called from behind a black cloth. I looked up, and 'click!' that was my picture taken. When we had the postcard copies they were brown, too, like the studio. Mum called it 'Sepia', but I and my pretty mauve frock came out white.

Some weeks, or perhaps months, later a man called at the door to ask whether there was a picture Mum would like to have enlarged and framed. Mum shewed him this one. She pondered over what the man said, but said she really could not afford seven and sixpence. That was nearly a quarter of what Dad earned in a week. The man persisted and in the end she gave in. Dad was cross about how much it cost, but he liked the picture. It was big and in an imitation wood frame. It hung on our wall always, wherever we moved to.

When I was seven or so, Cinderella left the Playmates Club in the *Wellington Journal*. She was replaced by Cousin Kate. I wrote a letter of welcome to Cousin Kate, and entered some of the weekly competitions. I had a prize for a picture of three Alexandra roses, grouped the way the Master had shewn us at school. And I had another for suggesting a name for the dog on the badge. My choice was 'Faithful'. The dog was named 'Friend', chosen by the winner in the over-elevens section. Cousin Kate asked for a picture of me, so we sent her one of the sepia postcards. She published just the top of mine, saying, "This is Playmate Selina, taken at the age of six".

Next to the mauve pansy frock, my favourite of those Aunty Alice made for me was a specially crisp white cotton, with tiny, tiny orange rosebuds, and even tinier green leaves. The touch of it always made me feel clean and neat. And because I was not naturally gifted towards neatness, I used to long to stay the way I felt when the rosebud frock was clean on, all fresh and smooth. I happened to be wearing it on one of the brightest of all May mornings. Mum and I were setting out along the track to the farm, carrying the white enamel milk tin. Joanie's Grannie Beedles called to us from next door –

"They took her in last night."

"Oh," Mum was interested, "We didn't hear anything." After a conversation I did not altogether follow, it turned out that Joanie now had a brother and that Nancy, her mother had gone to Berrington to fetch him. They would not be home for a fortnight. Berrington? Hmm, so that was where brothers came from. I did so long for a brother. Strange, though, going in the middle of the night - and taking a fortnight? I had not pictured Berrington being so far away...?

We went on to the farm. The milk-tin was not for milk - we had that in the evening. Word had come that a cow had calved, - "So tell the Missus if she wants some beestins..." Of all the lovely things which summer brought, 'beestins' was near the top of my list. All we needed to do was pour the white swishing liquid into a buttered enamel pie-dish, stir in a bit of sugar, a few sultanas if we liked, but they were not important. Then Mum grated a sprinkling of nutmeg on top and placed it carefully in the oven. It didn't have to be a hot oven, just the warmth from a lowish summer fire. By dinner-time it was set into a delicious custard pudding. Next to those little Viennese shortcakes with the jam on top, my favourite treat from Morriss's van was a custard tart. A beesting pudding meant a whole plateful of the lovely custard without the labour of having to "eat up the pastry". Mum sometimes put the beestings into a pastry lining, but often the pastry rode up on top of the custard, so mostly she didn't bother.

Mum's cooking was, on the whole basic, adequate and wholesome, if to my mind less than creative. Her cakes were for the most part plainish, either with or without sultanas. I had eaten chocolate-cake, even seedcake (though I couldn't say I liked that) and other kinds when I'd been out somewhere, so I knew that things other than sultanas could go into cakes. When occasionally I was at home alone for a morning or so, I made some experiments. I could never tell why cocoa added to the basic rubbed in mixture did not produce chocolate-cake. I tried Camp Coffee when we had some, but that was disappointing, too. I had heard of teacakes so, desperate for success, I reached for the tea-tin. That solid lump of would-be cake made 'interesting' by a couple of spoonfuls of Golden Stream tea-leaves was, I think, the reason I gave up baking - for a few years.

Countryfolk liked to keep seasonal traditions. Mum always aimed to cook rhubarb-pie for Easter Sunday, and gooseberry pie for Whitsun. If the Church calendar was late, and the garden season early we might have new potatoes and peas for Whitsun too, perhaps even lamb in place of our regular beef. Then my job was to chop the mint - forever it seemed - until the bits were almost a powder and tiny enough for mint sauce, to serve from our special green jar with white glass lining.

Summer was really with us when Dad made his ceremonial first lifting of new potatoes. Tapping the worst of the soil from his boots at the door, he brought the bucket into the house. In spite of the fact that they grew every year, that seasons had never yet failed, there was an air of surprise, almost disbelief in the joy that the wonder had happened again! –

"Look at em, surree!" he smiled. "They'm beauties. They'm doing well this year." (He won prizes for potatoes at the Shrewsbury Flower Show in later years.)

Outside again, he scooped water from the rainwater tub with the wooden handled bowl-dish. With his hands he swished potatoes and water round and round against the inside of the bucket. He poured the dirt and the water back on to the garden and rinsed them again. Most of the skins had lifted from the shining smooth roundness and the rest came away in the fingers.

"Fetch us a bit of mint, Oot," he said to me, "and give it to Mamma to put in with them." He always called her Mamma, though I never have. Mum always insisted that we paused and wished silently before we ate the first of each crop every year.

I have said that time went slowly for us children. We were impatient for the first of each of the year's fruits. As soon as gooseberries became recognisable as gooseberries, we were scrumping them into pocket and sleeves and knicker elastic. They went with us everywhere, to school, on walks, in our play houses, even to chapel, and of course to bed. Dad always held unripe fruit responsible for my annual plague of impetigo sores, round my mouth.

We would have done the same with apples, except that custom, for whatever reason, had provided them protection, for a time at least. It was a strict rule that young apples were only fit to eat if they were christened by rain on St. Swithin's Day. So we children were in a dilemma about St. Swithin's Day. On the one hand, if it rained on 15th July it could rain for forty days and forty nights. Yet if it did NOT rain we were barred from tasting the precious new apples. It seemed half our lifetime ago that we'd last tasted an apple. We knew nothing about imported ones, for all we knew it didn't happen then. These hard, not even very appetising fruit were our only chance. We were getting desperate. It would be months before they were truly ripe. Talk about Eve's dilemma! What WERE we children to pray for?

Chapter Fifteen

Harvests, holidays and high days

Harvest fields

At what point do I begin to tell about memories of harvest time? For the gathering in from the fields was but a high peak in an almost continuous process, the Farm's perpetual reason for being. The land, the buildings, we people, the animals and the seasons seemed TO BE as related to those few weeks of squirreling at high summer.

All through the powerful green-growing months, we children followed the filling of stems and ears to full corn. We spent a lot of our own spring hours walking and sitting and thinking among the acres of it, not ON the growing crops, you understand, but around and along those few fallow inches of adlands. There we watched for birdsnests and for wildflowers, and we thought through the lengthening days.

Then, suddenly, one bright day early in every summer, quiet was shattered. The mowing-machine clattered its course first round the adlands, then steadily crunched through the suntipped grass and the clover.

Much of hay harvest went on whilst we were at school. Mum greeted me home:

"Dad's cutting in the bottom field. Sit a minute for a drink and a butty, while I cut up his tea. Then you can take it."

She'd probably been waiting for Mr Birch with the bread. She stood the round cob-loaf on its side, balanced on the flat where it had touched its neighbour in the oven. Splinters of crust flew off as she cut away the top end. We did not often have real butter, but advertisements told us that Stork margarine was as good. Even that cost ninepence, twice as much as ordinary margarine. So, when she'd tipped the block onto the dish, she laid the paper onto the cut edge of the bread. She scraped the clinging marg with her knife, and the springy bread sort of pushed from behind and that way she captured the very last smear off the wrapper. She saved the wrapper to line her cake tin.

I ate the first crisp crust with some jam as I watched her first spread and then cut the pieces from the loaf. I wondered how she kept them so straight, though substantial, the way Dad liked them. Then she pressed pieces of bright orange cheese between them. She boosted up the low fire with sticks to boil the kettle quickly. We had to be careful not to get the woodsmoke into the spout or the tea tasted horrid. She warmed the big glass bottle with some tea straight from the pot, then measured an inch or so of milk into the bottle, spooned in some sugar through a funnel she made of her curled hand. She filled the bottle with tea, twisted the cork tightly in with its rubber washer, then tipped the whole about a bit to mix in the sugar. The bottle was wrapped round with a whole newspaper. It could be that day's newspaper, for Dad to read while he ate his tea. His tastes in food were simple, but they were exact. Any variation in content or quality was not welcome. Above all he "simply couldna bide cowd tea." A round wicker-basket, tall with handles as high again as the base part, supported the bottle best and I could hang it over my arm. Journeys with Dad's tea really were all sunny, for that was harvesting weather. I can still smell the wildflowers and camomile crushed under my feet, as well as the fresh-cut clover as I followed the sound of the mowing-machine.

The partly cut field looked like a tablecloth, one of those heavy green afternoon tablecloths with a fringe, except that the fringe went on for layer after decreasing layer round the edges of the standing hay, the square getting smaller with each round by the horses. Cut stalk-ends of the felled grass felt bristly like a scrubbing-brush, and the 'fringe' part soft and seedy. When the waggoners had finished cutting, and the hay turned and dried, all available hands with long pykles transformed the flat fringe into haycocks. We were always warned about the sharp pykles, so mostly we played games round the cocks already made, had our own picnics there too.

Corn harvest followed, in July and August, even into September. Always oats were the first, then wheat, then barley. Corn was cut with a binder. Flat strips of wood went round and over, over and round, laying the cut stalks heads together, and tying them with hairy binder-twine into sheaves before dropping them in rows along the field, to be stood together into stooks to dry. Although there were a number of hay and corn-fields on Uckington Farm, I always picture corn cutting in the Side Field between *The Thatch* and the main road, always hay-harvesting in the 'Clover' field behind Number Six, and always carrying from the field down the Back Lane opposite Pughs and Wainwrights.

Dad and Mr. Luther carried in relay. As one was loading in the field, the other was unloading in the stackyard. We children had to time ourselves into the right places for the happenings. We followed the loaded dray up the lane, then watched the men passing the sheaves on the end of a pykle to other men who built up the stacks under the Dutch barns. The object of our being there was the ride back. It was a highlight of our summer to sit in a row on the floor of the empty flat-dray. The high ends which held the load in place shuddered without its support as the horses manoeuvred all through the gates of the stackyard, round the corners and down the bumpy Back Lane. If the ride itself was a treat, the company with us was truly fantastic. For, milling around on the floor of the dray, among the bits of straw and weeds, the odd thistle and crushed poppy flower were all the wriggly crawling dancing-around-in-circles insects you could ever imagine. The dray was alive with them. Earwigs, ladybirds, spiders, little flies, big flies, beetles of all shapes and sizes and colours – everything you could possibly imagine. The odd thing was, as I think of it, they did not sit and be carried as we did. Rather, they scurried around, up and down, about and beside themselves for the whole journey. They must each of them have travelled the distance to the field many times each on its own two - or four - or six - or eight - or more legs. We were not scared of them, as I remember. They were not the least bit interested in us. Simply they could not wait to get back into their field again. If I could choose to go back in time and really look at Uckington in the nineteen thirties, those insects on the harvest-dray are what I would first like to see again.

It was characteristic of Dad that he would not ride on a cart whether empty or full - nor on a horse. However tired he might have been, he always said that the "poor owd oss was tired to dyeth", and he "wouldna burden her with his weight."

In school holidays we set off for days in the harvest field, hopefully armed with stout sticks. As the square of uncut corn got smaller, excited, we closed in. The intention was to catch rabbits as they fled, their estate cut from under them. We put up a show of running to catch, but I knew I could never run fast enough. I sometimes wonder whether I could have bashed a rabbit if one had sat and waited for me. I certainly couldn't hit a rounders ball. But it was all part of our harvest.

Dogs were best at catching rabbits. Yet even Izzie sometimes found it all too much. Izzie was a border collie, a working dog. She belonged to the farm's Uncle Vin, but we were all very fond of Izzie. She seemed almost like one of us children. Sometimes we met her tearing away from the harvest field, with froth at her mouth, like a streak of terrified black lightening. They said it was a fit. She went like the wind and instinctively found herself a quiet place to recover. Mum always insisted that the reason those hottest days of late July were called Dog Days was that dogs found them particularly stressful.

In the cooler evening, Izzie appeared again, calm and rested. And in those hottest of harvest days, the man and the horses came up from the fields with the reluctant twilight and had scarcely laid themselves down to sleep, before dawn declared it was time to begin all over again.

Summer thoughts and visitors

At high harvest, with sun scorching clover, then corn, into ripeness, men and dogs and horses worked to drop.

Life indoors was a battle against flies and curdling milk and a heat you could sometimes scarcely breathe in. Dangling strips of gummed paper flycatchers twisted themselves between the ceiling and their little cylinder packets. Flies kicked their last there until each paper was full. Outside near the backdoor, sweetened water in a jam-jar lured wasps to drown. In real heatwaves beef could be 'off' before it got into the oven. A cured bacon-joint carried better. Mum boiled it over the dumpy paraffin stove, to delay lighting the fire. The cooked remains kept on the cold slab in the pantry under a wire-mesh cover.

Mum bought bottles of 'Mason's Extract of Herbs' from which she made a kind of beer to supplement Dad's tea-bottles.

Grown-ups talked about it being 'close', which puzzled me. Close to what? What was close to whatever it was? Since the expression preceded a thunderstorm, I concluded that 'it' must be thunder? I remember very little about thunderstorms as such, noise, lightning or torrential rain, though we children did ponder as to whether God was stamping His feet or moving furniture - or barrels? as we did as to whether snowflakes were really His goosefeathers. Thunderstorms have a grim part in my memory for a different reason altogether.

We had a piece of furniture which had dominated

our living-space since, probably, before I was born. Its proper name, I believe is an overmantle, but because we never had a mantle which was low enough, or a room which was high enough, ours always stood on the long sideboard cupboard. At Number Six, this was opposite the window. It had a prettily carved and turned wood-framed large centre mirror, with three more little mirrors each side and a curved row of tiny, tiny mirrors at the top. And all of the glass had bevelled edges, so there were innumerable reflections of all that we ever did in the kitchen as well as some of the outdoors. It more than doubled the room, yet it led us out beyond ourselves. Belief had it that mirrors, along with everything else which reflected, attracted the lightning. To leave them exposed when lightning threatened invited disaster. Even bicycle handlebars were suspect: folk told about how lightning 'played on them' so some people painted their handle-bars black. At the first suggestion of thunder, knives and scissors - and of course mirrors - had to be hidden from the searching lightning. A whole bed-sheet hung over our lovely mirror piece and the room we lived in died. The sight of the whole wall of blank sheet where the mirror was filled me with more terror than the storm could. Oh, the relief, when Mum said, "I think it's about gone over now," and we came to life again.

Although we slid on the pits when ice was thick, I don't remember paddling in Uckington water. But sometimes we went to the river. With jam pieces for our tea, a bottle of lemonade, towels, bathing-costumes and a rubber ring, we set out down the Back Lane. We crossed the Norton to Walcot road into the wooded lane through Smethcott, crossed a field to the River Tern, near Upton Forge, on the way to Upton Magna. Sometimes grown-ups came with us, but we were trusted to go alone. The river was shallow at high summer, but perhaps up to our waists. I floated with the help of the rubber-ring, but without it I got water into eyes, ears, nose and everywhere. That was the first time I went off learning to swim.

The way from Upton Magna has other happy memories, too. If, instead of following over the field to the river, you walked on and crossed it by the bridge, you eventually reached the railway station. As well as train journeys which I loved, and meeting visitors which I also loved, we were sometimes summoned by a postcard from the stationmaster to collect a parcel. Parcels were exciting and came from a number of sources.

Several groceries and other things had coupons, to be saved to claim a gift. We collected enough pinky brown cocoa coupons for my Brownie Box camera. Mum collected tea - or were they soap coupons? - for a lovely tea-set, white bone china with little green and black and gold sort of medallion pattern. It was our 'best' for years and years. All these arrived for us at Upton Magna station.

And again, there was not a lot of money to be spent from 1930s farm cottages, but was there competition to claim the bit we had? Perhaps the more cunning coveters were newspapers. Because of them I came to know the word 'canvasser'. From time to time there was a knock at the door. Mum described the man as a canvasser from one of the daily papers. What the man wanted was that we should stop buying whatever paper we had currently and change to his. If we saved the issue number from the top left hand side of the front page and stuck them with flour and water paste to a paper he provided, when we reached a specified number we could send them away for a wonderful gift. The gifts we had were always books, and books were otherwise not easy to come by at Uckington. So Dad frequently came home to dinner to find we now had a different daily paper. He tolerated changes between the *Daily Express* and the *News Chronicle*, though he preferred the *Chronicle* so we had more of their books. But he drew the line firmly at the *Daily Mail*. For reason known only to himself he absolutely refused it. Once Mum gave in to their canvasser. Dad was furious. *Daily What? Daily Blimmin Liar* more like! You see an change it back again - sharpish. I binna havin that here!"

We had lovely *News Chronicle* books, especially a needlework one, with beautiful stitches for knitting and embroidery and a transfer which I used for a cushion cover with different shades of lilac flowers. Their *Everything Within* was the only real reference book we had, apart from their *Home Doctor*. From the *Daily Express* we had the *Boys and Girls Book of the Year*. That supplied dates and other information for school homework and it had pictures of the *Home Page Cat* which you could flick through fast to look as though she was moving. All of these came to us by a walk through Smethcott Wood from the station. The postman came that way, too.

A number of visitors came to Uckington in the summer, by train and otherwise. Some years a charabanc brought children from Wellington for a treat. They came from Tan Bank Sunday School. We did not see much of them on our Sundays at their chapel because they left for the main part of the service, but on this day there seemed to be hundreds of them. We tiny band of natives felt overwhelmed. They peered about them, looked almost unbelieving that we actually lived there. We considered them and wondered how in the world it must feel to live other than at Uckington. Great tables of food were on the big lawn and rounders and races were played in the corner of the Front Field, nearest the farm house. There were children everywhere. Then we waved them on their way again, never quite knowing whether we were glad or sad to have the place to ourselves again. They came and they went in a day.

At the beginning of August holidays, Joanie-next-door's cousins came to stay. They came from Sutton in Surrey, which we understood to be even further away than London. The girl cousin was another Joan, making three in tiny Uckington for that time. She was as different from us as it is possible to be. We were none of us very conscious of how we looked, but pressed for self description I suppose the picture would have shewn a tendancy toward earth-bounded-ness? Bright cheeks, firm shapes, even those less solidly built than me: hair from medium mousish to dark brown. We were not at all aware of our voices either. But this girl was tall, slender with a sharp clear profile. Her straightish hair hung smoothly, its colour somewhere between moonlight and the ripest sunbleached corn. At once casual and graceful, she moved with such ease that we felt like elephants. Fair as she was, her long limbs wore a suntan as leaves wore green. I want to say nonchalant, though I didn't know that word then. All I knew was that she made me feel I was still growing out of the earth, whereas she could undoubtedly fly. And when she opened her confident mouth, well...! That was the first time I saw her, on our doorstep at *The Thatch*. If she had spoken in Greek, she could not have been moreintriguing or more mysterious.

"Hellew," she piped. "Ken yew cam erwt to ply?"

I fear I stared for longer than was polite before answering this fascinating herald from an England so very far beyond Shropshire!

To Pankymoor

My own holidays away began at Shrewsbury station.

"Is anyone going to Wem?" Mum asked the people in the railway-carriage. "Would you mind seeing that she gets off there, please? There will be somebody there to meet her." Then she had a word with the guard.

Adventure was in the steamy noise and the smoky smells. When the platform began to move away, it was wonderful: the strange back views of houses and factories - and the wrinkled leather strap over the brass button holding the window fast, and the pictures over the seats. As we got near to Yorton station I could see Grinshill Hill. Most summers we walked there from Pankymoor. I knew that the other side of Grinshill was Preston Brockhurst, where number 38 was the first house I remember living in, and where a gooseberry bush grew from a hole in the side of an apple tree; where there was a low wall I used to walk on when I was three, and where Mrs and Miss Parrock still lived next door. Some holidays we walked from Wem to Preston Brockhurst to tea with them.

The glory which Wem was for me began with a rainbow next to a signal-box. For it began with Eckford's field at Tilley Crossing, a field consisting of rows and rows of sweet peas. Mum always said, "Look for Uncle Harold among the sweet peas," and mostly he was there and waved at the train.

Next there was the field full of cows in front of Granma's house on one side and the Mill chimney and the town on the other side of the railway line. Granma or Aunty Ede was always waiting for me with Doris, (my cousin Doris was a few years younger than me. The big square waiting-room was only the first stepping-stone on our mile or so's walk back to Pankymoor. The man who took my ticket was only the first smiling person who welcomed me back to Wem year after year. For what was so different from Uckington was that there were so many people and shops in Wem; and what was so different from Shrewsbury was that Granma knew all the people, even those in the shops, by name. And they all said how they wouldn't have known me from last year, for hadn't I grown!

I can't remember all of them, but Mrs Shone sold sweets and ice-creams, Mr Sands sold shoes, a different Mr Sands sold tomatoes, and our friend, Miss Edie Williams with a soft croaky voice, sold us groceries from Mr Edge's shop. Earlier years I think we had met her at Hunters' shop. Mr Rhodes sold shaving-soap and razorblades, Mr Morgan sold cough mixture, Miss Burrows sold cups. Mrs Strong sold me a writing-pad to write home to Mum and Dad and a reading book which Granma said would keep me quiet. Another Miss Williams sold us stamps at the Post Office.

Mill Street had to be crossed half way down because the footpath changed to the other side of the road. Wem Mill chimney was a landmark in my week there, I suppose as the Wrekin was at Uckington. I used to twist strips of paper round my fingers, then stretched the curling, easing it out into a mill chimney. Beyond the Mill the street became Park Avenue and it was here, under the long Grove School wall with the letter-box, that I practised my pavement steps. For I walked many times to Wem during my stay, and pavements were a novelty. Instead of walking to avoid the lines, as people are inclined to do, having in me a streak of what Dad called 'pig-yeadedness', I did the opposite. I stepped on to the lines, and even on to where the lines would have been if the stones had been laid side by side instead of alternately.

Right in the corner by the railway bridge and Mrs Cheshire's fence was a little hillock, covered in grass except for a path over the top, ritualistically trodden away by all the children who passed.

"Walk towards Shawbury Road until you can see what's coming!" Granma always warned us, for you simply had to look three directions at once to cross at the bridge.

In Shrewsbury Road we might see Mrs Maudsley, we might call for eggs. We would certainly see the sign which hung on her house, Pankymore Villa, and which said, 'Teas with Hovis'. Past the red wall of the Oaklands, the white gate into Pankymoor field had a different fastening from other gates I knew. You put an arm round a piece of iron which went upwards. You had to pull it open from a catch at the top. We looked for the milk. Mr Roberts from Loppington left it in bottles under the little hawthorn tree, except when it was paying day. Then he drove his van over to the houses and treated Doris and me to a ride back over the field. Sometimes he took us on to Tilley Green and even as far as the *New Inn* before leaving us again at the field gate. Granma and the aunties used to leave galoshes under the little tree too, if the grass was wet or the path by the pit was muddy.

Pankymoor Cottages were two joined together, with a tall hedge surrounding both, a wicket-gate each, and a pump in the field halfway between them. After carrying water the distance we did at Uckington, a private pump seemed very advanced.

Aunty Mary, Uncle Harry and Doris lived at Number Two. Granma and Grandad, Aunty Alice and Uncle Harold and Aunty Ede when she was not living-in at Mrs Keeble's, and Aunty Nance when she was on holiday from Birmingham, all lived in the other. Mr Kynaston had an extra bedroom and sitting-room underneath built on for Granma's big family – so I understood.

One thing which made it so very different from Uckington, was that I could remember moving to Uckington. But all of our Farlow family seemed always to have been at Pankymoor. Certainly Dad and his brothers and sisters had been born there, perhaps even Grandad and his family, too. I felt as though our family had come to be, simply by growing out of the lovely place and its atmosphere.

By the time I knew her, Granma seemed tiny and frail, yet she had borne and cared for six children on very little money, and had done a lot of other things, too, so she must have been strong. Her fine white hair was curled round a pretty soft face. Her dresses had low-cut square necks, into which she set a lace modesty vest, with a frill against her neck, and red or pink glass beads. In my mind I always link her lace and beads with the beaded net cover they kept over the milk jug. She and I shared our name because we also shared our birthday.

By the time I knew Grandad he was bent low. For if you saw him at work he was invariably carrying a sack on his back over the front field, towards the Show Field, or wherever the cows needed it. When you saw him at home his back was still bent almost the same, for it had got beyond being straight again.

I absolutely loved Pankymoor. It had all been together so long, house and people and furniture and things, that the things seemed almost to breathe as the people did. The long polished dresser had shelves full of willow plates, and a tiny house which when you got close, turned out to be a missionary box. The dresser-drawers' handles made a little chinkle sound at mealtimes because the folded tablecloth lived there. And always, always, because I was there in August, a formal vase of tall, straight sweet-peas breathed their fragrance into the polish and the lovely cooking smells. Uncle Harold grew sweet-peas at home, as well as working at Tilley for the Eckford family who were famous for sweet-peas. Uncle Harold was also responsible for the wireless. Only he ever turned it on or off, and he disconnected the aerial at night - in case of lightning.

The Grandfather clock stood high as the low ceiling, its rhythm like a heartbeat. A laboured wheeze, as though taking a deep breath before striking the hour, seemed to confirm a personality which had guided generations of my family. Only Grandad himself handled the clock, and although it was checked with Big Ben every newstime, it was corrected only on Saturdays when he reset the enormous weights. The high mantelled fireplace had room inset for chairs beside its blackleaded hobs and the oven. On its wall at the back hung a row of polished brass ornamental firetools. I sat in the hobseat and tried to beat the shiny poker gently against the wall to chime in time with the clock's striking.

Shelves of bright lustre jugs and things hung just inside the door. Aunty Alice dusted these and the furniture every dinner time before she cycled back to work. Of all the family, I felt closest to Aunty Alice. She was a tailoress at Mr Pye's shop. When they had extra work, for a funeral or something, she brought some home to do. I loved watching her sew. Most of all I was intrigued by the almost geometrical fashioning and construction involved in tailoring, and the sort of 'reasoning' which governed the shaping.

Most of my holiday spending money I took to Bowens for a piece of crash, perhaps a transfer, and embroidery cottons to see how much I could achieve by the time I went home. Granma knitted vests, twelve inches long in knit-two-purl-two rib with sixty stitches on number eight needles. She brought pretty pink wool from the chapel. The vests were for black babies in Africa.

Down the garden path at Pankymoor, by the lilac bush, was the *Houses of Parliament,* plural I suppose, because Aunty Mary's one shared the internal wall. This was something else which was different about Pankymoor. Instead of ordinary newspaper such as we had Uckington, they had their squares made from the *Radio Times.* So my education was extended accordingly. My first introduction to classical music in particular with such strange and unpronounceable names, came through those pages. The mysteriousness of the language of music and of the miracle which the wireless itself began to penetrate my mind together through that mid-day twilight from the not quite shut door of Pankymoor *'Parliament'.* When Granma became very ill, Aunty Ede gave up Mrs Keebles, and stayed at home to do what Granma normally did. Even when Granma was better, Aunty Ede stayed at home to help her. It seemed to be expected. She was a little lady, too, rather like a second Granma. Her hair was already white by the time I first knew her.

Granma had a number of friends in Wem whom I had to visit every holiday. Mrs Cheshire by the railway bridge wore long black clothes and a hat, even indoors I think. Mrs Jones was shorter and rounder, a happy lady who lived in Wemsbrook Road. We reached her along the path by the Castle field, where they had the carnival. One year at Carnival time I quite felt I was going to be squashed among the crowds along the Castle Walk. Mrs Davies lived at Barkers' Green and had a piano and an organ which she allowed Doris and me to play. I especially liked to visit Mr and Mrs Arger who lived upstairs at the back of their antique shop in the High Street. She found me books to read, and gave me one by the poet Longfellow, with purple pansy flowers on its cover.

In the evenings, Uncle Harry came round. He sat in the hobside seat. Sometimes he talked quietly and sometimes he just sat quietly and smoked his pipe. We were on the whole a quiet family. We didn't always have to talk when we were together. Perhaps it was the quiet peacefulness that made the memories sink in so deep. My stay must have caused a few problems. I was not at all good about going to bed. I tried my best to delay it until the grownups went. I shared Aunty Alice's room, mostly her bed. And as I lay with my ear on the pillow, a noise w began quietly, then louder till it roared and was frightening. I came to know it was only a train. I knew, too, that it was quite safely on the railway line a whole field away, but as I lay in the Shrewsbury-most corner of the house, facing the wall, my ear was cupped so it sounded just as though the train were coming straight for me. I didn't mind if Aunty Alice was there. Sometimes, if all the aunties were home, I slept next door with Doris. We scarcely heard the trains then. We played word- games and kept each other awake for hours. Then the game became 'First one to speak is a donkey', and that way we eventually got to sleep.

It fell to Aunty Ede to take me home. Doris came, too, sometimes to stay at Uckington. Once we went to the Granada on our way through Shrewsbury to see Shirley Temple in 'Susanna of the Mounties'. Trouble was, Doris got afraid of the galloping horses and Aunty Ede brought us out. I was annoyed. Mind you, as Aunty Ede said, I always was inclined to be cross on the journey home from holidays. I suppose it had something to do with my being betwixt and between my two worlds. Yes, it was nice to be back home where I could make mud-pies again, and yet I think perhaps I was secretly jealous of Doris for living at wonderful Pankymoor all the time.

Home and harvest

The peak of the farm's harvest was high summer; harvest at home overlapped and followed on towards autumn.

The wooden ladder which Dad made stood among the fruit trees, disappearing under the drooping branches. Every evening till dusk and every dinnertime Dad's heavy boots and his trouserlegs, tied round with leather yorks, moved up and down on its rungs. When he reappeared, his hessian fruit-picking apron was lumpy with plums or apples or damsons. He tipped them carefully into round straightsided basket measures left by the dealers for that purpose.

"Mind what you'm doing! Dunna bang em or they'n bruise and we shanna get nothin for em then!" Dad warned. Stalks got stuck between threads and persistent leaves had to be separated. "They wunna pay us nowt for leaves!"

There is no picture which speaks of seasons quite like an abundance of freshly gathered apples with stalks still crisp and twigs and leaves clinging – or of crowding purple damsons with the down-bloom still on them. When all the basket measures were full, fruit overflowed into Mum's clothes basket, into wooden orange crates, tea-chests or cardboard boxes - even into the zinc fireside bath lined with newspaper.

When we knew a dealer was coming it was all-hands-haste to gather as much as we could, for while dealers collected demand was good and the price as high as we would get. What fruit was left, Mum and I would have to take by bus into town, either to a fruit-shop, like the *Shropshire Produce*, or to the Market. That happened mostly with damsons.

"The trouble with damsons is they'm either all or nothin!" If the frost or the wind or the rain or the bees - or even the wasps - did the wrong thing at the wrong time, the trees bore no more than a sprinkling - and the price kept up.

"Another year you conna move for em. The dealers dunna want em - they say they wunna shift..."

The damson money was an important part of our income. Mum might rely on it to settle bills. Dad could be measured for a pair of 'britches', his best ones brought in for work; and we'd be sure to need shoes. The year I passed the scholarship, certain items of my school uniform had to 'wait for the damsons'.

A glut and slump year could be heartbreaking, though; so much effort and energy and little or nothing to shew. One particular Saturday, Mum and I took the zinc fireside bath loaded with damsons into Shrewsbury on the bus. The metal handles bit into our sweaty hands as we lugged it between us up the lane. For some reason we were later in the day than usual. Either Dad had to finish picking them at dinnertime, or perhaps we needed to wait for his wages for the bus fare - perhaps both. The shops were open to nine or ten o'clock on Saturdays, but by the time we got there any demand which might have been for damsons was already satisfied. We bore our load up the few stone steps into the market and out again - into one shop and into another - and out again. In the end somebody said, "Give y'eighteen pence to take em off yer ands Missus!" So eighteen pence, one shilling and sixpence and our empty bath, we had in return for many pounds of damsons and all the energy we could muster.

Mum sighed – "Dad'll expect us to do better than that – it took us ninepence for the buz!"

And of the things we did not sell... Some of the damsons burst and then bubbled themselves into jam in a soot-crusted jam-kettle over the fire. Jars and sugar warmed on the hob. I wrote the name and the date on white paper circles, then spread flour and water paste round the edges before pressing them over the jars.

More damsons became wine, in a wide earthenware steen covered with an old sheet over a stick, and it was fed with yeast frothing on a round of thick toast. We'd made rhubarb wine earlier in the year. Then my job had been to feed the sticks through the mangle's wooden rollers.

"Crush the fruit to extract the juice," Mum's recipe had said, and she thought the mangle was as good a way as any. My Granma Farlow made wine with beetroot and she let me taste a little while I was there, so long as I ate a Marie biscuit.

The trouble with our wine Mum said was that it didn't keep. Not because it couldn't but because it didn't get the chance. It was all gone before Christmas. None of us ever got drunk on it, but we did have some giggly Sunday evenings.

Apples were placed, not touching each other, in wood or cardboard box trays, covered with bits of old sheet, or Dad's shirt tails, or cotton flour bags, and stored on top of, or underneath cupboards, the washstand or anywhere in the bedroom where space could be found. Through winter they changed their hard green rosiness to mellow gold. Those we did not munch along with our ludo games, eventually wrinkled. Upstairs the smell of them gradually mellowed, too. I have always associated the smell of wintering apples with bedroom fluff and chamberpots.

Between us we sliced mountains of kidney beans into stone jars. It was my job to crush oven dried blocks of salt, with a rolling pin to pack between the layers. We sealed the large pottery jars with several layers of stuck-down brown paper rounds.

At school, vases and jars on the window-sills became crammed with Michaelmas Daisies, dahlias and then chrysanthemums. Pockets became crammed with conkers, and we stuffed ourselves and stained our hands and mouths with new walnuts from the dewy grass under the trees in the lane by the Williams' house... And our school singing time became filled with the hymns and the litany for the harvest festival.

At home, an early crisping of the air found us holding thick pieces of bread at the end of a fork before a high gleedy fire.

"Crush the crusts with your fingers as soon as they're done," Mum said. "It makes them nicer to eat."

Dripping from our half-crown of beef melted on the hot rounds; the gravy-jelly from underneath and some salt completed them. With the first of the celery, this made our quick Sunday tea before rushing to the Harvest Thanksgiving.

Winter jumpers from the box on the landing had been aired in readiness on the line over the fire. Consciously cosy with the unfamiliar texture of winter on our arms and flashlights in our hands, we left well before six o'clock to walk to Wroxeter. In a feeling of adventure we took not the Beslow lane, as to school, but the middle lane to Wroxeter, which we knew best from car journeys on wet days when we bumped over the little bridge.

Now, in the new autumn an evening mistiness hung among the grass and the trees and the hedgerows. They settled, no longer crisp, but bending, mouldering towards winter. However early we started, we felt we must hurry, for the church was always packed for *The Harvest*. We were anxious by the time we crossed the bump bridge.

Even the dim lights of the church seemed bright after the outdoors. The colour and the smells of chrysanthemums and apples, the berry-branches and the corn met us at the door as our solid shoes clattered on the pitted stone floor. We squeezed with Joanie and her family into one long pew. Often I had the first tickling cough of winter at about that time. I had to struggle with it throughout the service. So, for all the school rehearsals and my practising at my staircase services, the frog in my throat got in the way of the harvest hymns. Always it seemed the joy and the praises had to pass my throat as a croak, especially on the high notes. Yet I cherished the pictures in the words of those hymns. The golden fields, in the ripening sun, the grain all full with the soft rain - and the angels with their spiritual 'reapings o'er', mingled in our minds among the pears and potatoes, self-consciously draped with autumn leaves on the sills under the stained glass windows. All of the year's countryside seemed to be assembled or symbolised there in Wroxeter church. Its smells were blending with the building's ancient mustiness, into a precious essence of time and of seasons, of history and of the present, of being, and of place.

Truth to tell, it was more than my cold which got in the way of my singing. For this was the peak of emotion in my whole personal year. The hymnwriters placed so much which was wonderful into their lines. When it came to "The valleys stand so thick with corn that even they are singing!" the vision of those golden singing valleys was too much. My chin wobbled, my voice squeaked, and streams blotted out the *Ancient and Modern*. I still have the same trouble with those lines, and my heart still has to swell with moist and silent praise. Pictures in the mind sometimes seem too powerful for words.

High Days

With 1934 a new word came into my life. Many did, but in particular the word *'Episode'* takes me back to where and when I first heard it.

By my ninth year, I was moving along the Big Room at Donnington, sitting somewhere just beyond the fireplace. The year had not long begun. Over our frosted feet, chapped hands and lips and chilblains, thirty or perhaps forty pairs of ears pricked as the Master spoke - in his specially important occasion voice.

"There is to be a *Shropshire Historical Pageant*, for a week - in July."

From the depth of our winter, July might have been the next century. The time and the circumstances were beyond our imagination.

"There will be incidents from fifteen centuries of Shropshire history - depicted in five episodes!" He spelt the word out for us on the board. "The first episode will be about Caractacus."

Ah, now... We began to respond for every one of us in the Big Room knew about 'Caradoc, a chief of the Britons, known to the Romans as Caractacus.' We had read about him, listened to stories and written about him, some of us more than once. At our school, the History of England began with our local Caractacus. 'Car-ac-ta -cus was a brave war- rior. He es-caped from the Ro-mans to the moun-tains of Wales....He built a fort on the top of a moun-tain which has con- tin-ued to be called Mount Ca-ra-doc to this day...' and so on, we had read - and had written.

"*The Pageant* will be held at Ludlow Castle," the Master was explaining.

Ludlow? I knew it to be somewhere beyond the Stretton Hills. Buses left the Square in Shrewsbury, when the Inspector called out, "Charch Strett'n n Ludlerw!"

Through spring and summer the whole county seemed to be involved with little but the pageant. The papers shewed pictures of the costumes, told about who would be wearing them, and, the stories within each episode and which some schools would perform. I have explained that we Donnington ones were not gifted at drama.

Everybody in the county who was ANY body in the county had a part in the production. The cast, truly of thousands, glittered with landowners and other dignitaries. Uckington's own Lord Berwick of Attingham played the part of the Bishop of Worcester. The Master taught us about the Poet Laureate, then John Masefield, who was one of the guests.

Looking back, it seems strange that there were no arrangements for all the schools to go. We heard and saw so much ABOUT it that we almost felt we HAD been a part of it. I expect some children went with parents, though I can imagine Mum, looking at all those famous names, deciding it was not really intended for "the likes of us". The Pageant raised thousands of pounds for Shropshire Hospitals.

We did see some of the performers in their costumes, though, at other events, on other high days. Every year we went to Attingham Garden Fête. Usually the Master gave us half a day off to attend. Once, when he refused, I rebelled and went home anyway at dinner-time. I have told that I could be wicked. We caught a bus to the Mytton and Mermaid, then walked respectfully under the elaborate gates and the stately trees, along the drive through the park. This was to me an almost ritual pilgrimage into that world of fête-spelt-with-an-'ê', important enough for me to play truant, to be among the people and to experience that other-worldness which was symbolised there at Attingham Hall. A number of the attractions did not appeal to me - like running races, (Why did summer events always include races and fizzy pop? I much preferred coffee - or tea, or milk.) The strange hot-rubber spice smell of the *'Motor Cycle Spectacular'* always reminded me of the crash on the corner at Preston Brockhurst, when we lived there. The greasy pole to be climbed for a pig, the sweating, grunting man-strength in the tug-of-war bothered me somewhat. I wished they would let me be with the beautiful place and all the people, without having to enjoy the entertainment, except for when the *Pavanne Dancers* from the Pageant. When their stately dances were over, we could stand close to them with their unbelieveable hooped gowns, almost like double crinolines. Gliding over the grass, the fabric rich and silky, the colour of foxgloves, they could have stepped from the best and most colourful of books.

Some days, perhaps a Bank Holiday, or another specially brilliant summer day, Mum said -

"What if we take our tea up the Wrekin?"

A bus set us down at the lane end which pointed to the Forest Glen. From the Forest Glen there was an uphill wooded walk before the clearing where the swing-boats and the café and the lavatories were, before the climb began in earnest. After the swing-boats, which I liked more than anything, what I liked most about the Wrekin was that you never saw the whole climb at once. Over every ridge which looked as though it was the top till you got there, another was revealed still to aim for. It was as though the climb had been planned in manageable portions to encourage us.

At the top we fearfully edged ourselves through the Needle's Eye, concentrating on the rocks we trod on, trying not to think too much about those towering narrowing above us. I felt the time had to come when I should be too big to get through. What if it happened suddenly, say as to Alice, whilst I was still on my way through? Even so it was a testing to endure at every visit.

The view from the top was of course partly what the

climb was about, yet perhaps I, at least, appreciate it more in retrospect. For horizon hills and the wide spaces were part of our own everyday landscape. So the Wrekin summit provided what we expected: our own surroundings, though much more so - more so even than Grinshill and to a different scale. Yet because then I knew no other landscape, the world might all have been like that. Perhaps I had not yet properly learned to wonder. It was my mind's-'scape', though, for when, in those forty 'lenten' days in the wilderness Satan took Jesus up the mountain to tempt Him, I always pictured them at the top of the Wrekin.

Highest of all of Shropshire's days had to be the *Shrewsbury Flower Show*. Not many people from Uckington could afford to go to the *Flower Show* in the 1930's. Any adults who might, did not consider it a place for children. Even so, we children enjoyed those bits of the *Show* which came to us, so to speak. Harvest-fields took a back seat for that Wednesday and Thursday in mid-August. We organised ourselves with lemonade and pieces to the high bank along the roadside in the Front Field, that bank which I called Alice's. The object of our being there was to watch the cars go by. For a time we might try to count them in the continuous stream, but in the end the numbers beat us - so many shapes and colours which until *Show Day* we'd only seen on cigarette-cards.

At the end of the day, with gathering dusk, grownups and children arranged ourselves on to the five-barred gates near the stack-yard. We were always much too soon and had first to watch the sunset, impatient for the shimmering colours which succeeded it from the fireworks. If the wind was right, in the evening quiet, we might even hear some of the distant bangs. After, from my pillow at Number Six, I watched over the landing and the darkened field and fell asleep counting the cars' lights homeward.

If the *Show* was for adults, *Shrewsbury Carnival*

was for everybody, on the third Thursday of every September. Pavements were tightly-packed with a continuous jumble of people to watch the procession. Memories are of craning necks, of willing them to show us round elbows, between shoulders and heads, and of straining from feet stretched and on tiptoe to see the walking acrobats and fancy dress. It was there that I was told about periscopes, though we never had one. The floats shewed up better over the crowds. Millions of blossoms escorted the Carnival Queen and her retinue which I believed to be princesses. Millions more flowers made up pictures of advertisements or fairy-tales or songs. The characters on the lorries held out long poles with buckets on for us to throw money in for the hospitals. Elves and clowns and piccaninny cotton-pickers badgered their way among the crowds with more buckets thudding with money for the hospitals.

Among the procession, between the floats and all the fancy dress came bouncing and swinging armies of 'jazz bands' and troupes of dancing children from each part of Shrewsbury and its suburbs and from other towns. Bursting with neighbourhood pride, they vied with each other in brilliance and precision. The children in each group pranced in order of size, from tiniest tots to almost grownup like the big children at school. And yet these were not like children at our school at all. For we were a motley crowd of fifty or so between five and fourteen. Only here did we ever see so many children together, whole rows of them exactly the same. In their paint-coloured satin, shining, metallic in the sunlight, each was the spitten image of the others. A tiny drum-majorette led each band, twizzling her swizzle-stick, and each of her followers either had drums to vibrate, or a metal bazooka through which an indescribable sound played the very best and brightest of popular tunes, if with limitations. I practised for ages afterwards with a comb and paper.

In the year of the *Pageant* the Shropshire Yeomanry

took part in the procession. We stood along Mardol Head, near Hilton's Shoe shop, excited because Joan and Barbara's Uncle Vin was among them. I had seen his lovely hunter in the loose box and the field at Uckington, but this was different. The riders were dressed in historical uniform, tanned faces, stained red and fierce, and frighteningly warlike. I found that horses on the farm were one thing, but a streetful of these sweating brown giants turned my skin to gooseflesh. Their towering heads and the din from their clopperty feet resounding round the buildings could have been cannon-fire. From my place a few rows back on the pavement, those magnificent horses were fearsome.

When the procession had passed, the whole pavement turned and began to move towards the Quarry to watch the dancing and the tableau displays where the shiny children competed for prizes.

Once when we were leaving for home, long after dark, we stopped to watch a proper Dance Band. The music was piercing and coloured lights flashed from the trumpets and trombones. Players and instruments hopped and danced all at once, and somebody sang –

"HOLD the TI-GAH ... HOLD the TI-GAH".

That song belongs for me at *Shrewsbury Carnival*. There always seemed to be a bus home, however late we stayed.

Hold the Tigah

Hold the Tigah

Chapter Thirteen

Looking Away

Firedance

Somewhere in the middle of the nineteen-sixties I came across a particular poem. It was my pondering over its meaning that first began my reminiscing about childhood in Shropshire cottages. The next few pieces are set around its theme, that of *'Looking Away'*.

'The Self-Unseeing' by Thomas Hardy.

Here is the ancient floor,
Footworn and hollowed and thin.
Here was the former door
Where the dead feet walked in.

She sat here in her chair,
Smiling into the fire;
He who played stood there,
Bowing it higher and higher.

Childlike, I dance in a dream;
Blessings emblazoned that day;
Everything glowed with a gleam;
Yet we were looking away!

'The Self Unseeing' ... More than any other poet, Thomas Hardy has a way of taking me by the mind, and reliving with me the scenes of childhood: his childhood - and my childhood. For a timeless spirit of place and relationship is the essence of many of his poems. His floor, if it can be

seen today, still tells the same story: that we value today more highly as it becomes yesterday. As our memories reshape the shadows into the people we once knew, we begin to acknowledge their worth.

So it is that the worn away hollowing of a stone step or a floor has me dreaming as to its fashioning, and to those lifetimes of footsteps. Where were those feet going to - or from? The faces above them, radiant confident faces, some cautious, seeking, questioning - others worried, weary, sad?

How were the footsteps? bustling and businesslike, or furtive, frightened, faltering steps? Painful rheumatic steps, helped by a stick, and children's first explorations into the outdoors, whole generations of feet from midwives to coffin-bearers have carried away and destroyed an undetectable fragment of floor. Silent history calls from an ancient stone or quarry tiled floor: no wonder some places are felt to be haunted.

The floor and the music and the dancing in the Hardy poem from the first time I read it have led me back to Uckington.

The scene is the kitchen at Number Six. It is early evening in either spring or autumn. Dad is outside gardening, either planting or harvesting. Mum is helping him, perhaps picking up potatoes. Or she might be chopping up logs into sticks for morning and filling coal-buckets. She has banked up the fire with slack to empty the coal-buckets. As daylight from the window fades, and the Wrekin and the fields and the sky become one and the same in the deepening dusk, the fire gradually brightens and the room becomes lit up with firelight...

A gramophone with a horn was a new joy. We bought it for ten shillings, complete with a large cardboard box full of records, from the Lewis's. They were the family who had followed us into *The Thatch*, and they had "gone over to the wireless" as people were doing then. We were thrilled with the gramophone. Dad's favourite records were the brass bands and the comic songs. Mum liked what she called "sentimental ones". But when I had the room to myself I liked to clear the furniture back baring as much as I could of the red tiles, and choose records I could dance to.

I had seen dancing on rare visits to the pictures, like the Empire's children's birthday treat, and at the Granada Christmas pantomime. Then there was that tiny plaster couple which Joanie's mother set on to their records at Christmas when they invited us in to tea. Round and round the couple glided and they swayed with the music as the record turned.

I think it must have been the cinema which most inspired my dance, for I felt my stocky shape change into something altogether more expressive - like Ginger Rogers. For I twirled and I twisted, I stretched and I bended, bowed, swooped and lifted to the bendy swoopy music as a voice sang 'Carolina Moon', 'R-i-i-i-o Rita' and 'Ramona' and a lot more songs. Most of the songs that I played were about lonely people calling for, or about, someone. One man sang a song called 'Down the Lane to Home Sweet Home', about when he was a lad back home with dear old Dad. A bit over the top perhaps we'd call the words today, but at eight or nine or so I had never come across heartache. Now here it was in the music and I found myself being the channel through which it flowed into the dance.

I began the dance on my own, yet as the firelight strengthened all my movements were doubled and redoubled into the shadows. With the multiplicity of the mirrors over the long cupboard, all was reflected again and again. What with the movement of the flickering flames, the room was alive with dancing and as full as any silver screen with movement. Sometimes I stood and sang the plaintive songs with the singer on the record and watched the firelight make its own dancing.

Mum came in with one arm round a box of wood,

and the other weighed down by a coal-bucket. We could hear Dad at the back door stamping, scraping and brushing the soil from his hob-nailed boots.

"It's nearly blind man's holiday," said Mum. "It's time we had some light on the scene."

That was her nightly expression, as she lit a paper spill from the fire. She stroked the wick of the oil-lamp with the flame. She polished the lamp-glass with a clean teacloth, and waited a moment or two before setting the glass into place. We watched the blue-edged point of light spread out evenly along the wick. The glass always misted at first, but already the room was changed. A tiny yellow moon shone on the ceiling above the lamp, and gradually the whole of the centre of the room gave way to the lamplight - and the fire flickers drew themselves back to the grate. The shadows settled themselves into the corners, for the glow from the lamp never quite reached here.

The kettle, already singing on the hob, was pushed nearer to the fire as Dad came in.

"Ee, is that the time?"

He blinked unbelievingly at the clock.

"Surree the days is drawin out!" (or "in", as the case may be). "An yer got any tea made?"

Sing us another one

Whilst the table was still full with gramophone and records, say after my firedance, we went on to play more. Then we shared the choosing and the winding up and changing the needles: thin like a pin for the quiet tunes, and thick to make the most of the marches.

Dad whistled along with *'Flash of Steel'*, the music sounding like its name, and *'Washington Post'* and *'Punjab March'*. We must have worn away a little more of that floor with our feet. We tried our best to "Sing like the birdies sing" as one singer sang that we should, and we "Painted the clouds with sunshine". There were some big records with bright red labels called *'Rhymes and More Rhymes'*, *'There was a young lady from wherever'* when we joined in the chorus – "That was a cute little rhyme,

        Sing us another one, do!" - and of course he did.

   Some of the comic ones were funny, with Randolph Sutton and Sandy Powell and a song about a shirt factory in Barcelona, and *'Down in the fields where the buttercups all grow'*. A few made me feel uncomfortable, somehow, and I tried to avoid them.

   We collected a number of records about Rusty and Dusty Brown.

      "Rusty Brown's come to live in our town,
      He's got patches on where he sits down.
      He's got a dog and Dusty is his name –
      Rusty and Dusty Brown."

I think they all began like that and each went on into one of their adventures. Strangely, the one I remember best was about their creeping under the big tent to watch the circus. Strange to me, because when once I went to see a circus in Shrewsbury, I did not particularly like it. I felt circuses to be another of those things that children were expected to enjoy.

   We bought our Rusty and Dusty records from Woolworth's. Another boy who came to us that way was Master Jimmy Fletcher. He had a sweet young soprano voice - I had not heard the like - as different from the boys at our school as it was possible to be. His voice cut deep into my memory, not only for its quality, but because of the songs he sang, and what they told about people's lives at that time. Again, perhaps some of the pathos was a bit overdone, but the words expressed an ache which many people truly felt. For untimely death featured. Uckington was too small a place to be typical, yet everyone there at least knew children whose mothers had died while those children had been tiny. The *Wellington Journal* told us more, and about horrifying suicides of men who had been depressed - or in debt – or lost their jobs - or even all three - beyond bearing it.

Even children could die. There had been the diphtheria epidemic for one thing; and for another, every one of us in Uckington had known Peter, the Taylors' grandson. He had been pale and fair and even looked like a child angel before he died at four years old during a tonsils operation. So the weepy songs gave expression to a genuine sadness.

Those of Master Jimmy Fletcher's songs which I most remember were about a boy and his father remembering Mother:

"Are the angels singing to Mother?" and another called 'Daddy':

"Take my head on your shoulder, Daddy,
Turn your face to the west.
It is just the hour when the sky turns to gold,
The hour that Mother loved best..."

I expect the comic songs tried in some small way to compensate.

Most of our records from the box we had with the gramophone from the Lewis's were old when we had them, and belonged as songs to the 1920s or even earlier, rather than our 30s. Some had tiny excise stamps stuck on them. Florrie Ford bounced into my life this way. Her bright voice, her accent which I later found out to be Australian simply bubbled over. Even she could nearly make me cry though, with 'A Bird in a Gilded Cage'. Then I had a dreamlike vision of a golden birdcage with a golden bird standing in a corner with long gold wings - and a sad girl's face.

Another of Florrie Ford's songs was about overcoming hardship, of hiding it with fun, all about a pretend party with pretend food and drink. Mum explained that just after the war a lot of people were very poor indeed and some truly had nothing to eat. It was Florrie's bubbling-over liveliness which told it forth, and which taught me a lot about feeling things. I can remember how I wondered about *'Living on air'*. We played it so often I can still remember the words. I can't promise the right order:

"Money's tight everywhere
Now we haven't a bob to spare -
Stoney broke, it's no joke,
We've been living on air.

So all of you come to the party,
Jolly old pals of mine!
You'll find a welcome that's hearty,
And where the cooking is fine!

There ain't no mutton or beef or pork,
But help yourself to a knife and fork,
And let's pretend
We're having a jolly good time.

There's no ale or porter,
But what do we want with wealth?
We'll all stick to water,
To keep us in jolly good health!

And if you're famishing, don't you wait -
Just scrape the pattern right off your plate -
And let's pretend
We're having a jolly good time!

And when you've finished up every plate,
Then all you fellows can say your grace,
And let's pretend
We're having a jolly good time!

Time is short, home to bed -
I can see you've enjoyed the spread.
Hope the beer you've had here

Won't get into your head.

We've all tomorrow before us:
Parting is only pain.
So let's all join in the chorus -
And shout all over again:

There ain't no mutton or beef or pork..." etc.

I said we sang with the records. Yet never in the fifty or more years that I knew Dad did I hear him sing a note. Dad whistled everything. Marches, waltzes, popular songs, hymns - anything with a tune he whistled with the mastery of a blackbird. Birdsong, too: he echoed the tunes of those birds with whom he shared all daylight hours in the fields and the garden. It seemed to me he knew not only their songs, but their individual voices, could tell between a blackbird from one hedge and one from another. I truly believe he held conversations when there were just them, him, and the horses. A lot of people whistled, of course, yet I am sure Dad was especially gifted.

He had a particular feeling for the peewits. They were constantly round the cropping field and it bothered him that he was often the cause of their distress, when the machinery he was working with damaged their nest on the ground.

Then he packed up the grey, mottled eggs into a precious bundle in his handkerchief. I'll never know how they survived in his pockets. Sadly he unwrapped them for us: "Er wunna come back for em now, not once they'm disturbed. er conna in any case - the poor owd nest's all jiggered up."

The proverbial ill-wind brought us a treat. Fried, they were small, shiny and tasted rich.

It was Dad who bought most of our new records. He went "into Salop" some Saturday nights, perhaps with the harvest money. Once in particular, I can remember lying awake in expectation in my bed at Number Six. If I kept my room door open I could see the lights of the ten o'clock bus moving away from the end of the lane. A few minutes more and I would know - had he brought it? The front door opened and shut. HAD he? In little more time than it took to wind up the gramophone, the music floated through the echoey stairway and then the singing - a man's soft voice (Dad said Gracie was too expensive). The man sang:

"'Twas down where fisherfolk gather
I wandered far from the throng,
I heard a fisher girl sing
And this refrain was her song...

Red sails in the sunset, way out on the sea..."
Then Dad joined in... whistling.

When the table was not in use for meals or housework, it wore a dark-coloured between-meals cloth, perhaps heavyish damask with a tassle fringe. It was a background to homework, writing letters to family and friends, and to filling in football coupons, fashion competitions and crosswords, for our fortune - and to cards and other games, for our fun.

I suppose much of our fun was 'sponsored games' of a kind. I had colouring books and jigsaw puzzles telling me of the goodness of *Oxo* and of *Symington's Soups*. Our *'Snap'* was played with C.W.S. cards with a Wheatsheaf on the back and a product like *Pelaw Polish*, or *Waveney Peas*, on the Snap side. The healthiest-looking families peopled our *Happy Family* cards, all fed of course on *Cow and Gate* foods. The games came in parcels sent to school for distribution to us children. As advertisements they were lost on us, however. We never came across C.W.S. except on our cards. With very few exceptions, processed foods did not feature in our home-bake meal-times. As for tinned milk...! to our family, as to most country people, such things confirmed our opinion about what we understood to be 'urban deprivation'! An occasional tin of salmon or peaches or pineapple chunks was a treat for when someone came to tea. Then Mum made a point of keeping the tin for a few days as evidence – "Just in case..." she said. Well, you did hear of things...

We enjoyed the excitement of a new parcel and the smell and the feel of new colour-print and paper, even though our response was not what the senders intended.

Some evenings the kitchen table was the scene for our *Ludo* and *Snakes and Ladders* games. Mental sums of the dice-throws stayed in my mind as usefully as the Times Tables we chanted at school. And Dad taught me to play '*Fives and Threes*' dominoes, the same as he played at *The Horse Shoe.*

Mum brought armfuls of mellowing apples from the bedroom store and there might be a taste of new wine.

Boots and shoes

"They'm lettin the wet in. I sh'n atta mend em, I doubt."

I was always glad when Dad said he had his boots to mend. If it was soling and heeling, it could be a long job, and I might be allowed late to bed.

On a cobbling night, Dad sat forward in his high-backed wooden-armed chair, Mum's pleated hessian 'rough' apron, sewn by me at school, tied round his middle and over his waistcoat. Dad always wore his shirtsleeves rolled up, even for 'best', under his jacket. His forearms were permanently the colour of ripe walnuts. He gripped the heavy foot-iron between his knees, a boot resting sole side up on one of the slippery metal 'feet'. The soles and heels of his working-boots were patterned with worn-away nail heads, perhaps a quarter of an inch across. They had been square and as deep: now they sat smoothly on the soles in concentric horseshoe shapes, meeting in a line at the middle. Dad placed the V-shaped end of the pincers handle under an old nail, sent it 'home' with a sharp tap of the hammer, then prised each nail to loosen them. Then he gripped with the pincers and pulled them out, one by one, like rows of old teeth. The worn leather, lacy with the pattern of ragged nail holes, was peeled away.

The new leather, in texture and colour a bit like a sheet of rich creamy toffee, was cut to approximate size and shape from its parent square, then fixed, in the first instance, by carefully placed rivets. Before I could spell, I had used to call them ribbits, and I got teased about that. Now the leather was tailor-fitted, its edges smoothed and perfected with a special pointed knife. Dad clenched his teeth, and between held breath and his panting, the leather squeaked, and then shone where the knife pressed into the thickness and pared away the spare.

The places for the new nails were first plotted with the point of the 'nawl' (that is the 'bradawl'). It felt good to watch the horseshoe pattern build up again with the silvery cubes of the new hob-nails. Wider studs or steel tips went at the toes and heels. I stood, fascinated for ages, watching Dad's hands as he deftly struck each bit of the pattern home. On his fingers there was usually a cut or a bruise or a blood blister at some stage of healing, his fingernails black at the tips and jagged from the work that he did. Yet his nails were set deep along his fingers and darkly pink, with paler halfmoons. When we talked about them Dad said they were supposed to be filbert-shaped, and we looked and compared our nails with hazelnuts.The Master at school had clean square-tipped fingers with soft skin and shallow nails, not at all like Dad's with the moons deep along the fingers.

Sometimes the boots needed stitching. Dad reached for a small ball of coarse white hemp-thread. He drew a long piece, then pulled the thread again and again over a lump of hard resin. He called the new waterproof thread 'tachin end'. He gave it a cat-whisker needle which went easily through the stitch holes, into back stitches, sewing the leather layers together again. A final flourish to the whole procedure was a kind of melted wax stain on to the cut leather edges, presumably to seal out the mud. Bootmending could keep Dad busy well into the night, for he had to wear them next morning,by six o'clock - or even earlier in the summer.

His working-boots were expensive as our expenditure went. Boots seemed to be as important as the plough to a waggoner. Dad absolutely refused to consider wellingtons in any circumstances. As well as being "slippy owd things - you eerd such tales! ..."

"There was a chap in the *Horse Shoe* a tuthree weeks ago. He was sayin' about a bloke he knew - a neighbour of his. Gardnin' this chap was, shiftin' muck into his trench. He slipped a bit or summat, lost his balance whether or not - and stuck the yelve right through 'is wellington and into his foot! Took 'im to the Infirmary, any road up. They treated it pretty serious like. They ses as ow you can get lock-jaw, doing that..."

Dad drew in his breath. "Ooooh, no! I dunna reckon nowt on wellingtons. I udna wear em if they paid me to! - An I reckon they mek your feet cowd an all! I daresay they'm alright for some folks – but they binna any cop for farm-work - nor gardnin'!"

Mum's and my shoes had to be as tough as their cost would allow. "A nice pair of serviceable shoes please, not more than five shillings," we asked of the assistant in either Playfairs or Olivers. These Dad mended as long as he could, but sooner, rather than later - cheap shoes came to disaster. Gloomily he pronounced, "I canna do much about these: they'm shemripped." The sole and the top were irreparably parting company. Though he did his best with temporary stitching or rivetting, the need was replacement. Disaster was hardly too strong a word, for an unbudgeted five out of a weekly thirty or so shillings took some stretching.

For winter, Mum insisted that I wore leather boots high over my ankles. Remembering her own childhood, she considered these to be proper wear for me over the fields and the lanes to school. Sometimes the boots had buttons as well as, or even instead of; laces. I remember the struggle to fasten them with the button-hook. Some of Dad's boots and his leather leggings had buttons. The hook was as essential as scissors in our household equipment and it hung on the nail under the mantel-piece, which nail it shared with the line where we hung the clothes to air.

Shoes and other bigger items came mostly from the harvest overtime money, or the damsons, or from the pig at Christmas. My requests for fancy things were resisted - except for once. Then, I had a pair of black patent leather shoes for some special event.

These were not from a shop. They came about because Joanie's mother had a catalogue. The book was thick and brightly-coloured, with thousands of pictures of clothes, furniture and bedrooms with shiny curtains and eiderdowns and things I had not dreamt existed. The letters on the cover spelt 'Great Uni-ver-sal' and Joanie's mother said she had become an agent. She had to have twenty members to run the 'club'. (She'd have trouble finding twenty adults in Uckington). Each member paid one shilling a week for twenty weeks. Each was given a number between one and twenty. That number meant the number of weeks you had to pay before your turn came up. When it did, you had the catalogue back to order whatever you chose to the total cost of one pound for every weekly shilling.

I don't remember what else we bought that way, but I do remember my shiny shoes. They didn't last ever so long, however. We cleaned patent shoes with *Vaseline* to delay the cracking. But before long the fabric did crack. Then my shoes became as though made of black handkerchief cotton covered with shiny crazy paving.

Then even that peeled off. There must have been a lesson there.

Ploughing match

It was whilst we were at Uckington, that Dad began to take part in Ploughing Matches. It was a part of his character that he could not merely carry out the duties and skills which made up his everyday life - and ours. Annual repetition along with the seasons was not enough for Dad. That part of him demanded that each season's effort should produce better than the last's; so his whole energy went to developing skills towards the closest he could reach to perfection. To this end he did battle with 'Owd Nick' in the form of weeds and pests and diseases, and with drought and with flood and the occasional blizzard throughout the fields and the garden. In this cause he bore the frustration which was the bane of rivalry, whether with his own best so far or with other people's best. Then all of our spirits had to ride the crests and the falls of his ambition. Over the years his gardening, from shallots to sweet peas, from perfect round potatoes to four foot long leeks, was aimed at THE best. So with his ploughing...

Encouragement came during our first winter at Uckington, in 1931, when he won Third prize in the *Waggoners' Class* at Atcham and District Ploughing Match, held that year at Acton Piggot. He struggled over the next several years, getting mostly a third, occasionally a second prize. I believe his first First Prize even came after our Uckington period. He always met a particular friend, a 'ploughing partner', Mr Jack Onions. They ploughed side by side in the same class, until Mr Onions won First Prize, then he had to compete in the *Championships Class*.

Atcham Ploughing matches usually came at the end of January, and Cruckton and District held theirs around the end of September. Dad never travelled for any other reason, but ploughing took him to a number of other parts of Shropshire. Before the days of annual holidays for farm-workers, he had first to negotiate the day off from work - talk about a 'busman's holiday'! Then, if it was too far to take his Uckington horses, he might borrow a team from some farm nearer by, often from Churncote when the match was Ford direction, and he had to arrange a lift for himself and his plough.

Always the Sunday before the match was 'Survey Sunday' when he cycled to have a good look at the ground. It found him, with his bicycle, leaning on the gate, summing up with his shrewd eye the texture and the quality of the tilth. He would turn that soil over in his mind and all his senses as it rained or shone between Sunday and Thursday. The Sunday after the match the competitors were there again mulling, or muttering, over the judges' verdicts.

As well as the actual ploughing, Dad was keen on the *Turn out* competitions. This meant the horses were judged by the way they were turned out: their healthiness, their grooming, their dress - yes, their dress, or perhaps more accurately, their jewellery. For over their heavy leather collars and the rest of their harness they displayed their finery, and this is where Mum and I came in... and we came to be 'looking away' - like in the poem.

We covered the kitchen-table with newspaper and one by one Mum reached down the horse-brasses which hung over and around the mantel-piece and the long ones from each side of the fireplace. After a quick rub with the duster, we all set to work on them. We polished every fraction of every inch of each strap and each portion of leather until it gleamed extra, and each brass stud and each buckle until they shone like stars on the black leather sky. We lifted each heavy brass medallion, carefully covered the leather, then rubbed the brasses hard, backs as well as fronts, with *Brasso* and a great

145

deal of 'elbow grease', which Mum said was more important than the polish.

"Mind you dunna miss where the straps go through. The judges always looken there most particular!" Dad warned.

The pictures at the centres of the medallion shapes became old friends as time after time I laboured over them. Some had horses' heads, some sheaves of corn, some geometrical patterns, others I took to be some kind of farming symbols -- hardly any two were exactly alike. When polish and polishing were out of the way, and my hands scrubbed, I hunted among my knitting for the nicest wools to make into thistle tassels to put on to wire stems. The horses wore these twined into their plaited manes and between their ears, sometimes with ear caps I'd made for them to keep the flies out. We cut bright braid ribbon into lengths and cut the ends into fish tails. Dad plaited the ribbons in with their manes and tails.

For all their magnificent dignity, Shire horses had a reputation, especially when they were young, for being sensitive. Sometimes, while they worked or grazed near the main road, a sudden noise like a car back-firing could send them to bolt in panic. Sometimes they ran out of the field and it took a lot of time and patience to catch and to calm them. Yet they did not seem to mind the dressing-up. They walked and stood at their noble best whilst the *Turn Outs* were judged. The winners had an extra rosette to be added to their finery.

They ploughed at their best, too - seemed to understand it was special. The field measured out into equal strip sections, each ploughing team was judged by the straightness, the sharpness and the evenness of the finished portion. One by one, the furrows turned, each chocolate-coloured pleat laying against its neighbour as crisp as though it had been ironed there. So it had, in effect, by the gleaming slicing ploughshare.

By this time there were already some classes for

tractor-drawn ploughs. Waggoners looked on those with suspicion: "noisy owd things for a ploughin' match". Some said the ploughing was different altogether - that "it wanna 'ardly ploughin', somehow".

One year, a Ploughing Match came to Uckington Farm. Most of it took place in the field which we called the Clover Field, down the back lane and stretching behind the Patch Field which was beyond the Taylors' garden. We children had a day off from school to go. The Master said we must write about the Ploughing Match instead. Besides the ploughing and the turnouts, there were classes in pulling sugar-beet, and what interested me a lot – hedge-laying. I loved the way the men wove the long branches between stakes so that the hedge looked like a ribbon woven out of growing wood.

It would be nice to tell that Dad won a prize that day, but my memory got caught on a conversation. What I remember best is walking along the adlands in the lowering sunshine, though it was a bit wet underfoot. I was walking with Mum and some of my Wem aunties who had come over for the day, because it was so special. And I remember what they were talking about - the aunties were explaining to Mum about the matter of eating toffees with false teeth!

Perhaps the aunties' concern was to encourage, perhaps to warn Mum. For as long as I could remember Mum had joked about a widening gap between her two front teeth. She laughed about its being 'lucky' – "When I can pass a sixpence through endways, I'll be sure to be rich - that's what they say!" She could even have passed a halfcrown between them before one by one the teeth began to fall out. It was something to do with her gums. Riches were reluctant, though. Even replacement teeth took more than ten years, coming eventually with the National Health Service. Until then Mum went on joking about her gummy smile.

Remembering November

It is in that brilliant sunshine of deepest autumn, when the lowering rays penetrate further through the shedding leaves, that I think most of when we played at *The Bungalow*. To get there we went down the Back Lane. Somewhere beyond the Pughs' and the Wainwrights' houses, we could cross to the right through the stubbled remains of a harvest-field. Or we could continue to the end of the lane, turn right before Smethcott Woods and find the Bungalow about a field's length along the road towards Walcott. Its once white-washed walls and its shaggy, once thatched, roof shewed through the trees and the shrubs of its one time garden. The door creaked open. Small casement windows allowed in only a little of the sunshine between the trees around. A house without stairs intrigued us. I have wondered whether we borrowed its name from fashionable new estates in town, or whether it really had always been *The Bungalow*. For this was old - as though people hadn't heard of stairs when it was built. Now it was dilapidated, said to be unfit to be lived in, though people had lived there recently and still would in some family's emergency. Later, the Beedles family took over the land and the buildings for a smallholding and kept cows there. We took to buying milk from Joanie's mother when she brought it to our door in a small churn, measuring out our portion with a straight-sided 'silver' measure with a hook, which she hung over the churn's rim.

It was during *The Bungalow's* in-between times that we children had the run of it for our pretend housekeeping. It was lovely - had all the real things, like a brick washing-boiler with fire-space, and tiny door beneath; and kitchen range fireplace with an oven. We didn't light real fires there - or did we? - I think not. But we played our games in the real rooms with the shady corners, where even the autumn sunlight couldn't reach - and with all those feelings and the mystery smells because people had so recently lived there – ashes from their fire in the ess-hole, and their rubbish on the mixen outside. What fixed *The Bungalow* so firmly into my autumn memories was the pear-tree, absolutely loaded with pears, small hard reddish pears dripping from its branches and falling on to the wet grass like showers of rusty tears.

We were walking up the Back Lane home in the late afternoon of almost winter, in that extra stillness which was starting towards mistiness. We were passing the gateway to the Clover Field, when we heard the sound. A slow rhythmic labouring thump thump thump thump was reaching us from over the fields behind us, from over and beyond Smethcott Woods even. We'd heard trains in the distance for years, had ceased to notice them. Now - each puff hung onto the stillness around - this did not sound like a train.

"What's that noise?"...

"No, trains don't sound like THAT!"...

It got louder and heavier, a bit faster - and CLOSER! I think it was Barbara who said their Uncle Vin had been reading in the paper at dinner-time about something mysterious called the *Loch Ness Monster*. *Loch Ness* meant nothing to us, but *Monster* that noise could be. We quickened our steps home, with our own ideas about where - if not what - the *Loch Ness Monster* was. We knew for certain that it existed down in the direction of the railway line at Upton Magna.

Autumn in the farmyard brought friends Sam and Ned for the extra work there was to do, like when it also brought the threshing-machine. We heard its trundling approach down the lane, great metal wheels crunching the pebbles and the grit, over the farmyard into the stackyard, right along to the far end roughly to the back of the stable-block and, appropriately, near the Chaff Room. The rumble and the chuffing of the engine was a sort of musical background to the farm's activities for the few days it stayed. It was all hands help like at harvest-time. The corn stacked under the barns was now brought out and fed through the enormous hopper at the top of the threshing-machine - and what had been one commodity became three. Hessian sacks caught the bared grains as they poured from the chute; those full sacks which were not driven away in the farm lorry went to be stored in the granary above, which I described earlier, the one which smelt like inside a flour-bag. A golden mound of husks grew under the machine before being carted to the big pyramid in the Chaff Room. Then the empty straw went back under the barns to be used for winter bedding, and such-like – not to mention our pretend houses.

I suppose if the cheeping of chicks and the bleating of lambs told in their way the awakening of the farm's year, then the sound of the threshing-machine signified a 'tucking- up' of the harvest the object of the exercise. Not that the season really rested the farm's work. It was just different. If spring was for sowing, summer was for growing, autumn for storing, winter was for using - among other things.

Work went on in the fields, too. It was one of the year's landmarks, that, when it was darkening by around four o'clock and I arrived home from school, instead of the house having an afternoon feel and my dinner kept covered from mid- day, the kitchen still smelt of freshly-cooked dinner: Dad's used plate still on the table, and Dad still there with his final cup of tea, leaning over a bit to catch the fire-light to read the paper. I liked this warmer welcome, and the cosiness of the changed routine. It was brought about by what was termed 'One hooking'.

It meant Dad had been ploughing or whatever in a field a long way from the farmyard. So, instead of returning with the horses at dinnertime, and spending time un-hooking them and harnessing them up again, as well as the journeying time, he stayed in the field. Then he carried extra bread and cheese, and an extra tea-bottle.

They went on working through to something like a 'Three o'clock dinner' so that all the stable-work could be done in the hours after dark. 'One hooking' days have comfortable memories.

It was in winter that Dad had his accident. One Sunday he had been to visit a friend, Jim Kynaston who lived at Brompton, near Cross Houses. He usually went about mid morning and got back for dinner, if a bit later than usual. When he didn't come home and Mum said his dinner would be all dried up in the oven, we got worried. Eventually somebody brought him home in a car, his head bandaged up, and his face swollen. It didn't look a bit like Dad. He said he'd been cycling home down Cronkhill Bank and his wheel had caught on a sugarbeet lying at the side of the road. He was hurt all down his side too, and he cried out when he had to move. He was home from work for some time and the house smelt of liniment for his painful side. What specially interested me was a round cardboard tub of Green Soft Soap for washing his hair whilst the wounds were there.

The cost of doctors was a problem for most people then. We were privileged, because Dad's mother, my Granma Farlow, enrolled all her family in Wem Oddfellows' Society. For a small sum of money, each year members could have a free doctor, and medicine. Mum kept on paying for us too. I think she paid something like twopence a year for me, so we could all have Dr Gittins from Cressage when we needed him.

We didn't really like Dad to be ill, but there was something nice about having him home by the fire. I liked the feeling of differentness when Mum and I wrapped ourselves up on a dark night, lighting our way over the fields with Dad's hurricane-lamp to fetch him some beer in a jug from the *Horse Shoe*.

Remembering Novembers of my 1930s childhood is remembering often chill feelings of being less than content: heavy feelings, of being bothered in the mind about things not understood, of being disturbed to some measure, and not able to tell the right people.

At the end of each school day:

"Stand by your desks! Hands together eyes closed! Lighten our darkness we be-seech Thee, O Lord, and by Thy great mer-cy de- fend us from all per-ils and dangers of this night, for the love of Thine only Son our Saviour, Jesus Christ Amen."

Our tempo speeded up towards the end. What were the perils and dangers of the darkening hours of the closing year? Did we recognise our valedictory rites as a prayer in which we should trust?

Soon after the harvest hymn season was over our singing-practice took on a more serious tone. The Master began telling us about his time in the army - about the diet of 'Bully beef and biscuits' - about life in the 'trenches' - whatever that was - and the hard beds the soldiers had to sleep on. He spoke about "When I was in Mesopotamia - Messpot as we used to call it..." And he told about when food had been scarce in this country and when money alone could not buy sugar – "You needed ration cards, for a few ounces."

An oilskin map hung on the wall behind his desk and he pointed out places to us. Although Europe appeared to have been at the heart of what we then called 'The Great War', all of the bits coloured red scattered over the world had somehow to become identified in our minds with the sacrifice of our soldiers, and with national pride.

The Master named men "who were boys at this school, who responded to the call of duty that we might enjoy freedom." Freedom was not a word we would have used about school, but we supposed grownups saw things differently. We'd seen the names of some of those he spoke about on the memorial at Wroxeter.

We learnt all that we then knew about war at his telling, and he was convincing, for he chilled our flesh. As well as "O God our help in ages past" which we sang from our books, he copied a hymn on to the board for us to learn: "Oh, valiant hearts, who to your glory came..." He paced out the notes on the piano, a tune which went down deep, and twisted you round inside. We sang its many verses with true heaviness, for in our minds we went through the dust of conflict and through battle-flame, and we could all but smell the blood and the fire and the gunsmoke, and feel the ghastly mud under our feet. And we sighed for sorrowing families.

We Uckington ones had once seen soldiers. We had stood by the *Horse Shoe* one wet spring Saturday while hundreds of them marched from Wellington to Shrewsbury to meet the Duke of York. I had expected red soldiers like in toys and picture-books, but these were grim in sober khaki, with what I took to be khaki bandages wrapped round for leggings. The thunderous drum of their marching boots along the road struck somewhere in my stomach, and my legs felt weak.

Mum said she knew we had started practising for the Armistice Service one morning when she got up and heard me singing "God save the King" before I was awake. The Master said the the Great War had been called the 'war to end all wars'. Indeed, had we not felt that God was stilling all movement the world over whilst we stood for the two minutes silence?

And yet, grownups were beginning to speak in serious tones of things the papers were telling about happenings in Europe. Local papers had headlines about plans to build air-raid shelters. The mistress had told us over sewing that she and the Master would retire in 1939, the same time as Barbara from Uckington and I would be fourteen and, supposing we were still at Donnington, would leave school. Someone told me they stayed teaching longer because of the Second World War. Two names at least of those boys who sang with us were later added to those of whom we sang.

Armistice and Remembrance perhaps set the tone

for those feelings about November memories, yet my November-in-the-mind went beyond November-on-the-calendar.

The trail of that feeling of being disturbed leads me to Sunday afternoons when, for a time, we Uckington girls joined Uppington Sunday School. It seemed a long walk along the main road. If we felt naughtier than usual we might spend some of our collection pennies on the bus as far as Uppington Avenue. It was still a long walk under those trees, which looked like a tunnel until you got to where they seemed to meet and you found they didn't quite. It was not the fault of the vicar, who came from Belgium, that his rendering of the Anglican liturgy failed to impress my simple Nonconformist mind. But the disconcerting part of the memory was not that. It concerned a stranger who we only ever saw along the main road, a thin pale youngish man with fair hair and a yellow brown coat. Not every week, but sometimes he cycled past us as we went home. Then we passed him as he stood in a gateway, then he overtook us again and so on. He didn't speak, just looked at us. Once, he even followed down the lane to Uckington. We turned into the farmhouse drive. From the safety of the garden side of the big white gate, we turned and looked at him. He stood and sort of smiled a bit. Then he did speak. He said, "Don't be silly. I won't hurt you." In a few minutes he rode away. That was the last we saw of him. It was not a thing we felt we should tell grownups. I think we thought they might say it was our fault. He was a problem - then we forgot about him, well, almost.

Another shadow fell when I was sent on an errand after school to Wroxeter Post Office. Mum said, "Don't dawdle. Be sure to get back before dark - and don't speak to anybody. It says in the paper that Scarface has got out again." Scarface, I understood to be so far away, imprisoned for whatever he did, that he himself could be no direct threat to me. But, no! I didn't dawdle!

Sometimes I frightened myself. One evening I walked home the field way from Norton shop. It was safer because there was no path along the main road. It was that twilight time when shadows can take substance. Then a gently swaying blackberry briar can solidify in the mind to a potential threat, and a slender young elder tree into sinister human form. When such a shape had been safely passed and proved its innocence and harmlessness, I chided myself for having the audacity to have invented, simply by indulging my silly imagination, a whole new being. There it- he - had been, although only for seconds, and only in my mind, just set and waiting for me for some unimaginable purpose. It was as though, just for that short time, a complete person had been added to the world - simply by my thinking it. Who in the world did I think I was? - and it didn't end there. If I'd fabricated him, then he must have had mother and father - grandparents – perhaps brothers and sisters. He'd have neighbours, people would have known him, gone to school with him, worked with him. Oh, what a frightening thing I had done! I well remember reprimanding myself for being so irresponsible as to have created, by my stupidly thinking a bush into a man, all those other people of a person's existence. It did not prevent me from making the same mistake again, but I do remember my reasoning, and that hedgerow in whose shadows I reasoned it.

The famous 'Fifth' did not do much to lighten November for me. A few sparklers and Roman candles and silver cascades were cheerful in themselves. But the thought of the culprit Fawkes, whether alive or dead, being burnt year after year after year, I found grim, to say the least. Oh dear, November, what sombre thoughts you do provoke!

I lay with my scary thoughts in the dark after Mum said I was too big to need a light at night. One year I thought how comforting it would be to have my own flashlight to keep under my pillow. So when I said my prayers I began to ask that I might have one for Christmas. I was getting a bit old for writing to Father Christmas, too.

I did have a dark red, pocket-sized light, that very year. It was not among the things I opened on Christmas Day, though.

It was my present from the Christmas tree at the Sunday School party in the Duke's Room at Uppington!

Chapter Fourteen

1937 and new beginnings

We Uckington girls were thinking - dawdling about the long front drive of the farmhouse garden, when the word 'Scholarship' first passed among us. None of us was quite sure what it meant, though we felt it had some bearing on growing up, and for certain on foreign travel. Either was too remote for us to seriously contemplate.

Eventually the subject arose at school with the question as to who should sit for the scholarship. Those children who knew about such things supposed that what was meant was 'The County', which term we used loosely for the Shropshire County Council Education Committee School Entrance Examination, (no wonder we called it 'The County') which could provide free secondary education, depending on the financial circumstances of parents.

"Oh, no," the Master corrected. "Children from this school take *The Donnington Scholarship*."

I must explain about *The Donnington*, why there was an alternative. From round about the time of the Civil War in the middle of the sixteen hundreds there had been a history of education at Donnington for the children of Wroxeter and Uppington parishes. What had once been called 'Wroxeter Grammar School' (founded by one Thomas Alcock) moved from Wroxeter, probably the Church, via Eyton on Severn, into the big Donnington House. It became known as Donnington Free School. Eventually it declined and was officially closed in 1893. Donnington Church of England elementary school had been built on the opposite side of the road in 1874 with the Education Act, and carried on the tradition of providing education for children of the two parishes. A relic of earlier times remained in the form of *The*

Donnington Scholarship which awarded the winner twenty pounds a year to be spent on secondary education. The actual fees at somewhere like Wellington High School in the mid 1930s was around ten pounds a year, plus books and other requirements.

So those whom the Master selected to do credit for the school were entered for *The Donnington Scholarship*, and those whose parents were persistent entered for the County's entrance exam as well. I don't think Mum and Dad knew much about the intricacies of the educational system, but Barbara was the same age as me, and her family's interest helped us both to keep in step, as it were. (Joan was already in her second year at Wellington High School). Barbara and I were entered for both.

Sitting for the *Donnington* was education beyond the actual questions. For one thing we were among ten or so boys and girls from various schools. They lived in the right places of course, but some were already at fee-paying schools, like Kingsland Grange and The Convent. For another thing, the examination was held in The Shire Hall, then in The Square in Shrewsbury. What I remember most about the whole day is dinner-time, when what I remember most about that was having a disrespectful romp around the Court Room, among the polished, curvy-shaped wood, and standing in The Dock and reading the card from which the prisoner swore on the Bible. That was discovery.

The other exam, which I must properly call the *Secondary Schools' Entrance Examination*, was held at the actual school to which it was intended successful ones would go. Barbara and I found ourselves at Wellington in one classroom with, by Donnington standards, a whole school full of girls. A big day needs preparation. We washed my hair and Mum twisted it into curlers the night before. And I caught my regular special occasion cold overnight. So as well as my rebel hair tickling my face, it got tangled with soggy handkerchiefs, as I applied myself to the questions. Perhaps I was fortunate in having that particular year. For the main English composition was - "Give an account of arrangements being made in your parish for the celebration of the forthcoming coronation of King George VI". Perhaps we'd had a similar question at the Shire Hall, for the theme seemed familiar. "The arrangements being made in my parish to celebrate the Coronation are similar to those for the Silver Jubilee in 1935..." The arrangements had, of course, been made as well for the coronation of Edward VIII which had to be cancelled. I went on to describe those events.

It was a fact that we at Uckington found ourselves pulled apart somewhat on the matter of parish activities. For Uckington was in the Civil Parish of Wroxeter, the Ecclesiastical Parish of Atcham, its postal address was Upton Magna and telephone exchange Uppington. For such things as parish Christmas parties (and Coronations) we were expected to go to Atcham, yet because those were the only times, except for the Garden Fête, that we saw the Atcham children, we didn't particularly enjoy parish parties.

Between Easter and Summer holidays the results were made known. The *Donnington* was first, towards the end of April. The Master was pleased that of all those children taking part, those awarded highest marks were from Donnington. He explained that in the actual number of marks, my result was highest by two. But he had also to explain that the Trustees, having discussed the result which was very close, had decreed that, living as I did at Uckington, because for this purpose we were considered to be in Atcham parish, I was not eligible. Poor Mum was vexed: she never forgave the powers that were. And I think all of Uckington, such as we were, felt slighted.

"He shouldn't have allowed her to take the exam if she wasn't allowed to win," Mum went on. Yet, in the end, it did not matter to me, because in June we heard that I'd passed the other one. And already life was never again quite as it had been.

On our very last day at Donnington, Barbara and I were given some special personal sewing to do for the Mistress. We often were, but this stands out specially. She presented us with a number of coat-hangers, brought a fur coat to shew us what was required. We were to pad out the hangers at the middle so as to better support and protect the high fur collars. And what we had to use to pad them... I will not name, because they were things which, although we did, we were not supposed to know about yet.

So, a chapter at Donnington closed. A lot had to happen though, before another opened at Wellington. The list of school uniform was a shock to the family's budget. We were granted a maintenance allowance, which helped. Aunty Alice agreed to make my blouses and gymslip. The school had changed to the new shape gymslips which took less of the navy blue serge. Notwithstanding the grant and Aunty Alice's dressmaking, Mum said the prices at the special school uniform shop were out of the question.

"Three and eleven a pair for stockings! - a shilling a pair is bad enough. Seven and six for navy blue woollen knickers! Hmm. Not much if you say it quick, that's what I say! You'll have to wear ordinary cotton to start with. Then all being well when the damsons come I'll get you one pair of the others to wear for gym days. That's the only time they'll show." Mum didn't allow for the first morning when we lined up for the Mistress to check each item of clothing to be sure we had our names on everything.

More momentous than school uniform, perhaps even more than the change of school in itself, was that passing the scholarship brought me a bicycle, not as a reward for being clever, but of absolute necessity. It was the only means by which I could get the five or so miles from Uckington to Wellington at the times I needed to go. I had longed for a bicycle for ages, had at every possible opportunity tried to ride one, but had not yet learnt. So this summer's holiday at Pankymoor had special significance.

Cousin Doris had a friend, Isobel Kynaston. Isobel's father owned the farm where Grandad worked. They lived in the big house called the *Oaklands*, at the corner of Pankymoor field. She had a new bicycle, very modern, with a diagonal bar instead of the curved upright frame. It was because of Isobel's generosity in sharing her lovely bicycle with Doris and me that, after a week of constant practice, I went home from my summer holiday more or less 'field proficient' at least in cycling. The next thing was a bicycle for me.

My bicycle came from Mr Brayley. He lived at Wroxeter, and had a bicycle shop in Shrewsbury, near the railway bridge in Abbey Foregate. Dad had arranged with his friend Mr Kynaston from Brompton to ride home with me. I went with Mum on the bus as usual one Saturday and we met Mr Kynaston at the bicycle-shop. It was a straightforward journey home, with me riding on the inside, no difficult corners to tax me before we got to Uckington Lane. My legs revived over dinnertime, then there was no holding me. I needed to practice for the journey to school. Mum said I should go the back way at first, to avoid the busier main road. So Joan and Barbara and I explored the lanes round Walcot and beyond.

That was one of the greatest turning-points of my whole life. Suddenly the world became accessible. Places which had been at very least a planned walk, or a busride, or even impossible, opened up instantly at a thought and my own pedal-power, but not without cost in the beginning. I had become 'field proficient' on Isobel's modern low bicycle over Pankymoor fields. Yes... But...

My bike cost fifteen shillings, quite a lot for us, but it WAS second-hand, older-fashioned, higher, with bigger wheels and proportionately narrower handlebars - consequently it was less manoeuvrable. It and I took wide curves round corners - and roads and lanes were narrow after the field. I spent the whole of that first weekend on - and off - the bike. Once I fell on to the partridge place by the hurdles at the top of our lane. I collected one injury after another, mostly on my knees. Mum tore strips from old sheets. I took them rolled up in my pockets for first aid. People in the villages stared at my bandaged fast-driving knees. The more I knocked them and the more I pedalled, the more the bleeding came through, but I was determined.

It was in those early practice cycling days that Barbara and I set out down the Back Lane, latish one Saturday afternoon, to explore some of the places beyond Walcot that we had seen only on the way to Rodington or Marsh Green on Sundays. We meandered leisurely, following this sign and that. In what seemed no time at all we were near High Ercall. It was there that we saw the fingerpost: 'Shawbury – Wem'. Now Wem had meant holidays and train journeys. We were astonished to have come within fingerpost distance of that wonderful place - by ourselves - on our bikes! Elation got the better of us. Having come so far! - why not? There seemed no reason at all why not! So we did!

Granma was at once horrified and pleased to see us pedalling over Pankymoor Field on the evening sunlight. Sun always shone from over the railway at that time of day. "Deary me! You are so far from home, and it's not that long before dark!" My Granma Farlow had not reared six children without knowing what to do. "You must sit here quietly, and have a rest and a drink, and a tuthree biscuits, while I go over to the *Oaklands* and ask if they'll please ring through to Uckington Farm and tell Barbara's family where you are - and that you'll set off back directly!" Barbara told her the number. That done Granma reprimanded us. "You must never do a thing like that again: your mothers will be worried to death about you. Now off you go and hurry along home Pet Lambs!" She always called children Pet Lambs. That was the time when we began to learn about lighting up time and that there were legal requirements to cycling. We must have ridden at least twenty miles each way. What a heady freedom bicycles brought!

On 16th September, 1937 I arrived at Wellington High School for Girls wearing my navy blue serge gymslip, white blouse - and a tie! - and a Marks and Spencer red 'woolly' which varied slightly from the 'quality' regulation design, my navy blue felt hat with elastic under the chin, and its band with '*W.H.S.*' in red embroidery - and a gaberdine raincoat. That first morning was spent on the checking of parts of our uniform, copying out a weekly timetable ('Timetable'? -   Oh..., we'd never had one of those before) and receiving the first of a number of new textbooks. Then we went home. My first day at Wellington might have been my last, for as I cycled home through the town, I took a corner with customary wideness and missed an oncoming car by a hair's breadth. Term began with half a day, which was good because it was Shrewsbury Carnival day. And the day was memorable for another reason. That was the last I remember of my annual impetigo, for I never saw it again.

I must select for sharing only a few impressions of the new school. I was placed in Form 1P. No-one ever explained what the 'P' was for. Twenty-nine stands out as the number of girls in 1P, so presumably in the , to me, unnumbered other forms, with Uppers and Lowers and 'P's and things. The size of the building and the number of girls was truly overwhelming to a not very confident ex-Donningtonian bumpkin like me. But at least two from Donnington had preceded me, Joan Ryley, my Joan from Uckington, and Betty Childs from Uppington, and by now they were quite at home in the throng, so I took heart.

I was warned that Headmistress Ross could be formidable and strict, though she had a round pink and white face with silvery curls. A black academic gown distinguished her from the other mistresses. They mostly seemed to wear pleated skirts and knitted twinset woollies. Miss Ross took Form 1P for Religious Knowledge, which began with our underlining at her dictation the 'main points' in the Book of Genesis. At the same time she imparted a measure of elocution, succeeding at least in correcting my broad Shropshire 'TONGue' to a more acceptable 'Tungue' and our 'siNGiNG' to 'singing'.

For Biology lessons we were requested to take in rose-hips. All those years we had walked among dog-roses they had been commonplace, now that I rushed into town they became important enough to be taken for us to examine the insides of them.

We struggled with French pronunciation. Those strange exacting vowel sounds seemed equally elusive to those whose voices were as Shropshire had bred us as to those whom culture had groomed, and I met the word 'vocabulary'.

Second only to the size and numbers, what most impressed me at Wellington was the smell. Donnington smelt of chalk and carbolic and plasticine, with an occasional downwind puff from the fire. Wellington High School for Girls smelt of - cooking! As morning progressed the smell got richer and more hungry-making. Those people who knew about such things speculated with authority as to whether it came from liver and bacon - with onions? Hot-pot? Roast beef? Steak and kidney pie? - pudding? - and on Friday which kind of fish. At Uckington fish was fish - if ever it was - for it was rare. The deliciously tantalising smell was at its peak by the time some of us were queuing to collect our lunchtime bottle of milk. Each day we were eventually shewn the source of the smell. Then we had to pretend not to mind a bit that, as we sat one side of the long table, with plates provided for our home-packed sandwiches, those on the other side received plates and dishes loaded with food which looked as gorgeous as it smelt. I don't know how well we hid our feelings when some critical dainty noses opposite rejected the wonderful stuff. The problem was that school dinners cost ninepence a day, two shillings and ninepence a week which was beyond the means of many scholarship girls. We were learning that we came in categories. We might be girls, or plain scholarship girls, or free-book girls, maintenance grant girls and very rarely free-dinner girls. Then we knew that those girls' families were really very poor. I don't know which struck harder then: envy of the rich, or pity for the most obviously poor. But oh! the smell of those dinners!

Education came from and reached beyond schoolbooks. Morning and evening outside the school were fleets of school buses and streams of our girls poured into them. Place names I'd only seen in the *Wellington Journal* became real places where people I now knew lived. I'm not sure when I began to realise that, had I lived at say Dawley, or Hadley, or Oakengates... I might never have had that bicycle! And wasn't I the fortunate one!

Chapter Sixteen

Christmas at Donnington and beyond

"Marley was dead to begin with. There is no doubt whatever about that."

Nor was there any doubt whatever that, early in every December, the ghost of Marley would open our Christmas preparations, pervading the Big Room at Donnington, as though his phantom face had appeared on our classroom door. Day by day the Master rolled his ample voice over the deadness of Marley and of door-nails, round the clanging of bells and the clanking of chains. He revelled in dramatic repetition of some savoury passages:- "You may be an undigested bit of beef, a blot of mustard, a fragment of underdone potato. There's more gravy than grave about you, Eh - he! More gravy than grave - whatever you are!" The Master spat out 'HUMBUG's as if they burnt his mouth, and he grated at the meanness of Scrooge.

Day after day the Master fashioned for our minds the fog and the frost and the mystery of Dickens' London on Christmas Eve beyond our own imaginings. With Scrooge we were drawn by the spectre from bedknob to gravestones and into the Cratchits' family affairs. Scrooge's terror was our gooseflesh. Then we went with him through the joy of his transformation, and celebrated his reformation with that turkey. We could all but smell and taste the turkey, though few of us ever had.

Regularly as the season itself this was the Big Room's lead up to Christmas, a reading every day and we always got to the end at the right time.

The Infants' Room Christmas began with a list. The

Mistress dictated: "Listen carefully, and mind your spelling: Flour. Suet. Su-gar. Eggs. Cur-rants. Sul-ta-nas. Rai-sins. Can-died peel. Milk. Lemons... Ask your mothers which of these they can contribute towards our plum-pudding. You must tell me tomorrow, and then be sure to bring the items on Monday. Do NOT forget!"

Our little packets were emptied and weighed into a large pitcher-bowl. One of the children was sent to the School House with a note for Maud to supply anything found to be lacking. Maud had recently been at school, but was now in service for the Mistress in her house.

Such a stirring that pudding had. For twenty or so of us stood in line to take turns. Spices teased our noses as we prodded and lifted the mixture with the long wooden spoon. The speckled mixture looked strangely the colour of Peewits' eggs. Twenty stirs and twenty secret wishes with tightly screwed up eyes - and that was the pudding mixed. Last to go in was a number of silver threepenny bits, each tightly wrapped in paper. The Mistress covered the bowl with a crisp white cloth, then bore it away for basins to be filled then boiled in her copper. A few responsible children were chosen to carry the equipment and open doors and gates.

Outline pictures of flowers and holly leaves, birds on branches with 'Merry Christmas', or biblical texts, arrived on our desk-tops. New crayons too for careful colouring. We lined up for holes to be punched through stiff card at measured and marked positions. The punch and the paste were used only by the Mistress. We chose coloured ribbons for hangers and to hold on tiny calendars. Sewing days were given over to embroidering peg-bags or knitting pot-holders for our mothers.

Bright sticky paper was cut into strips to become paper-chains for the schoolrooms. But what I liked most was making paper lanterns. Each lantern began with a piece of plain paper, rulers and pencils, then our most colourful crayons, and our precious imagination. We chewed along the pencil lines with round-ended stiff-jointed always blunt scissors. We lifted the cut fringes carefully apart. Top and bottom edges rounded into circles, we held our breath as the lanterns stood. Their own weight opened up the spiky slats and the finished effect could not have been further from that original sheet of plain paper. At home I made lanterns of all sizes from oddments, even tiny silver ones from sweet papers. Imagination made up for candles inside. They were always my favourite decorations.

Scrooge, the pudding, the present-making, the lanterns... At Donnington as elsewhere, the other preoccupation was carol-singing. The words and the atmosphere of some of the carols came nearer to our experience than others. The *Three Kings of Orient* were... remote from us, I fear.

But there were days when light seemed never quite to break through, when the coldness of mist in the playground seemed to take on a presence, silently threatening as it froze our breath; when earth itself was hushed but for the echoes our shoes drummed out of the taut ground; and when the pit in Crow's field was so solid we could slide on it; when chilblains ached through shemripped shoes - and fingers screamed for warm gloves... On those days winter watched us through the school's high windows; and while we sang about ancient and mysterious *Bleak Mid Winter*, through our minds and through our bodies we knew, for we lived every letter of it.

One carol was our school's only excursion into Latin – if that is what it was.

"O and A and A and O, Sing cantimus in choro,
See our merry organ blow (or was it 'go'?)
Be-ne- di – ca-mus Do-o- o- o- o- o- mi-no!"
Were those really the words?

As for the day itself, Breaking Up Day. Party Day, Prizes Day...

The black, steaming, pudding was even more

special in the unlikely circumstances of its being served on saucers, and eaten with spoons brought from home for the purpose, to a clatter which replaced the thud of books on our desks. Its spiciness invaded the chalk and carbolic and plasticine smells some time during the morning. No need for concern about spoiling appetites, for breakfasts had been forgotten before we even got to school, and dinnertime pieces went down just as well into less than quite empty stomachs.

In the playground, dinnertime started earlier, and went on longer than usual. Nobody was allowed back into school until everything was ready, and the whistle blew.

As we nosed our way back into the classroom, the tree which all morning had been (almost) completely covered and had teased us with smells of Wrekin picnics, was splendidly revealed. So high that it towered on a line with the great window, its baubles catching light from the window and more from the fire's flames. Pink and blue parcels hung all over. In due course Father Christmas would read the labels: 'a girl aged ten', 'a boy of eight' and so on. Everyone had a present chosen for them by age and sex, names on this occasion being dispensable.

On each desk-top was a paper-bag, ends tucked in to hide for a little longer our tea: filled rolls, sandwiches, sugary, sticky buns, and a piece of cake. Again, part of the treat was the unlikely surroundings.

The Master's desk was transformed, set out with books which were prizes. The lady from Donnington House, always elegant in black, was there to hand out the prizes - to those who had attended, behaved and worked particularly well. A number of plum-red prayer-books were to be presented by the Vicar to some who had performed exceptionally. We peered from our seats, trying to read the titles, and if possible the names. Was there one for...? One year I was given 'The Big Book for Girls'. It thrilled me because I loved most of all to read school stories from the library box. Once, too, the Vicar handed me a prayer-book. That came in useful for my one-person services on the echoey stairs at Number Six.

We gave three "Hip Hip Hoorays" for the lady and the Vicar. It was understood that the lady provided our tea, and possibly the presents, and that the Vicar doubled as Father Christmas. We sang our best carols for them, then collected our apple and an orange to take home.

And our winter watched again as little convoys of us dispersed through the fields and lanes, winding their respective routes. It saw us loaded with prizes and presents and secrets in our schoolbags to be hidden from mothers until Christmas Day. And it heard us singing the carols again and again whilst dusk came and met us before we reached home.

I suppose what impressed me most about what was different about preparations for Christmas at Wellington High School for Girls was the music. A slim, dark-blue 'Church Hymnary', by denomination Presbyterian, replaced Donnington's 'Ancient and Modern'. I remember feeling that the tunes and the words were shewing me 'round the corners' as it were, of carols as I had known them, shewing me a gentler and yet deeper, more poetic dimension to the Christmas story - like this alternative beginning:

"While humble shepherds watched their flocks,
In Bethlehem's plains by night,
An angel sent from heaven appeared
And filled the plains with light..."

Filling the plains with light seemed to make Donnington's much-sung 'Glory shone around' seem almost commonplace by comparison. Another hymn on the same theme:

"In the field with their flocks abiding,
They lay on the dewy ground,
And glimmering under the starlight
The sheep lay white around,
When the light of the Lord streamed o'er them,

170

And lo! from the heaven above,
An angel leaned from the glory,
And sang his song of love;
He sang, that first sweet Christmas,
The song that shall never cease -
'*Glory to God in the Highest,*
On earth, goodwill and peace!' "

I think it must have been the picture of that angel leaning from the glory to sing his song of love which summarised for me that other dimension.

The Carol Service itself was a new experience, so many children - and their parents coming to listen. Joan from Uckington was not able to be there, nor her family, so Mum could not get. I was determined not to miss it, though I'd have to cycle home after dark.

The hall was packed with choir and audience and it was lovely when all the Christmassy sound soared over the frames on the high walls and among the climbing ropes on the ceiling. Head Mistress Ross was in charge. "Do NOT applaud them for their sacred work!" she admonished the few parents who sought so to encourage us.

The Carol Service stayed in my mind for reasons other than the music though. It was the first time I had cycled in the dark – and it snowed. We did not have a battery cycle-lamp then. Dad used a carbide one which consisted of a container, probably aluminium, the size of a large cup, which held chunks of carbide. The principle was that a controlled supply of water dripped on to the carbide and produced a gas to be lit with a match. The burner was contained in the top part of the lamp, and tiny green cut glass 'eyes' at the side showed from behind when it was lit. The front was a glass window/door through which the light shone. Well, the problem was that our lamp had been in an accident. At least half of its window/door was missing. The lamp still worked - in ideal circumstances. But on this night, as I said, it was snowing. I managed through the town to the junction of Haygate Road with the Holyhead Road. There was street lighting till then. Along the main road, I walked a bit and rode a bit and struggled a bit with the matches. But the wind and the snow won. Now country people in my experience have a kind of reserve and yet they can be relied on to ask and to respond at a time of crisis. So when at length I arrived at the Umbrella House, I knocked on the door.

"Yes, certainly," - they had a battery lamp I could borrow. I promised to return it next day in the day-light. So I pedalled safely to Uckington on borrowed light.

And what about preparing for Christmas at home? During the first week in December, dependable as the calendar itself, came Aunty Nance's parcel. Aunty Nance lived in Birmingham and her parcel was like a herald from some other world. When we'd all seen it, Mum put it away unopened until Christmas Day.

Shopping does not feature much in my Christmas memories. Money was as hard to come by then as the rest of the year. But each year one of the Saturday expeditions to Shrewsbury included a visit to a fairy grotto, or some such creation in the fantasy Christmas at Della Porta's or Maddox. It cost sixpence to see Father Christmas himself and bring away a parcel wrapped in plain pink paper. Had I been a boy, of course, the parcel would have been blue. There was intrigue in shaking and smelling and pressing and guessing, though its content was a bit hit or miss, in some generalised aim to please a universal girl with a flimsy and universal toy.

We spent some time at Woolworth's Christmas card counter. There were elaborate cards, all bright and tinselly, but we had to concentrate on finding the prettiest from a pile labelled three ha'pence each. They were mainly white, with cut pattern edges and little brown cameo pictures of sheep and things, perhaps a coloured sprig of holly. My Granma made me a book of glittering Christmas and birthday cards which people gave her after they had finished with them. She stuck them into exercise books and I used to award them marks and comments like "excellently beautiful", or "wonderfully gorgeous", but those we sent and those we received were modest. We posted them with a ha'penny stamp, or three ha'pence if we sealed them in with a letter. The postman began to arrive later in the morning and on Christmas Day he came as late as one o'clock. Then Mum gave him sixpence and a mince pie, and a glass of beetroot wine - if we'd been able to save any till Christmas.

Mum ordered extra currants, sultanas and raisins with stones in - and candied peel, whole pieces with the hard sugar clinging to them - from Mr Birch who came from Rodington with groceries and bread and next year's calendar. We put the fruit through the mincer for mincemeat and Mum got down the tin which had spices and things in it. We only ever saw the spices at Christmas, except in the summer for the beestings pudding. She always bought a paperlace-trimmed box of dates, and a pound of mixed nuts with shells on for us to crack on the stone floor with the flat iron. The almonds were always so hard and slippery we had to chase them under the cupboard where the dust was.

We might have chicken for Christmas dinner - and it might be the only one in a year although we lived on a farm. Christmas food was about what we didn't normally have. A few really hard years at the depth of the thirties we would not have chicken. Not that we went without. A 'nice piece of pork' could be cheaper. Then there was an extra joint of beef, our present from the farm. One Christmas Eve when I went with Mum for the milk we went into the farm's back-kitchen and they were all there... rounds of beef (much bigger than our regular half-crown's worth from the town), for all the farm-workers.

Making mince-pies was a job for Christmas Eve after tea. We'd not dream of eating one before Christmas

Day. Christmas was the day, not the weeks before it. Christmas Eve was for making mince-pies and putting up decorations. Two particular garlands looked down on our annual festivities. One was bright but ordinary. The other I've not seen since ours wore out, light green, a sort of intricate paper chain links, with coloured, pleated fans above and below the green at intervals. It was considered bad luck to decorate too soon, and holly was never allowed indoors even, before mid-day on Christmas Eve.

"Ooo -No! - terrible bad luck that'd be!" So Dad and Mum put up the decorations among the mince-pie smells. The focus of course was to get the house all special for when Father Christmas came. I knew the comics and everything said he came on a sleigh with reindeer and you never knew quite what time, but I knew better than that. I knew for absolute certainty that he came on the ten o'clock bus from Shrewsbury, and that was the time by which I had to be asleep.

Of the things that he brought, little things stay most in my mind, perhaps because they came every year, like nuts and tangerines and sugar mice in the toes of my school sock, and tiny bars of chocolate in different coloured silver paper tied with bright ribbon, a cracker and perhaps a rolled-up paper doll with clothes to cut out of the paper and dress her with. One year I had a beautiful china doll with black ringlet hair. I thought how sensible Father Christmas had been to ask Aunty Alice to dress her in a pink dress with tiny stitched pleats on the bodice. I named the doll Grace Olwyn, after two grown-up friends of Mum's who lived at Welshampton, Grace and Olwyn Thomas.

I have tried throughout my reminiscing about the nineteen thirties at Uckington to tell about things as they were and how they looked and felt then, and to avoid deliberate comparison with today. Now and again though, I've felt the need to look from today in order to appreciate a particular point. This is so now. Because what I value most looking back at Christmas then is that sense of quiet mystery over and throughout the place itself. As if what happened at Bethlehem was real enough and immediate enough to have happened, say in our own stables at Uckington. Going to bed on Christmas Eve, peering out over the fields in that absolute stillness and thinking... If the Lord had chosen Uckington... for that angel to lean from the glory and sing...in that perfect peacefulness we really should have heard him.

I've borrowed a poem. I don't think I'd heard of Thomas Hardy then, but this poem always takes me back to Uckington - and I know just what he means:

The Oxen
Christmas Eve, and twelve of the clock.
"Now they are all on their knees,"
An elder said as we sat in a flock
By the embers in hearthside ease.

We pictured the meek mild creatures where
They dwelt in their strawy pen,
Nor did it occur to one of us there
To doubt they were kneeling then.

So fair a fancy few would weave
In these years! Yet, I feel,
If someone said on Christmas Eve,
"Come; see the oxen kneel

In the lonely barton by yonder coomb
Our childhood used to know."
I should go with him in the gloom,
Hoping it might be so.

Chapter Seventeen

When Father turns...

Life and living seem to fall into patterns - long stretches of stability, then one big change followed quickly by another.

From 1930 life, far from standing still, progressed in an orderly way, seasons, years and experiences revealing and quietly enriching our growing minds whilst time gradually burst the rest of us through the seams of our clothes and the soles of our shoes. Seven or so years proceeded that way, Shropshire's horizon hills holding our world and our times in place.

Then as I've said, 1937 brought scholarship year, new school, my wonderful old-new bicycle, new companions, new ways of seeing - and of saying - things. As if that were not enough, even bigger changes awaited us round the turn of the year.

I don't know exactly when we were first aware of the impending moves. Knowing now how long such things take, especially in the farming world, I suppose there might have been a clue when Barbara from Uckington Farm didn't come with me to Wellington High School - that her family were perhaps already anticipating Lady Day 1938 (the quarter day when farm-workers changed their place of employ)?

In the meantime Joan and I continued our five miles each way cycling to Wellington, come frost or fog, hail, rain or sunshine. We became knowledgeable about the new 'streamlined' shapes of cars and new number plates. We pondered over GB plates, were sceptical of other children's theories that they meant Gone aBroad - yet what did they mean? It was ages before I knew.

Joan had often to take mysterious ingredients for cookery lessons, and to slurp home her Kilner jar of stew or something more exotic.

And new subjects continued to open up my world. We had music lessons regularly, every week at the same time - something I'd longed for at Donnington. The school's only male teacher came specially to teach us singing. He was very exacting. I was scolded when I pulled a face at the umpteenth repeat of a section of "Where e'er you walk".

I discovered an aptitude for the kind of reasoning exercised by Algebra, and I even enjoyed the way its problems fell into place; and I was fascinated by Geometry, where solutions involved relationships between shapes and angles. Strangely, though, arithmetic was less straightforward - fractions and decimals were all right, but I seemed to miss a cue somewhere in long division.

I took to early Physics lessons, the step-by-step observing and reasoning and recording of basic principles appealed to me, like those of thermos flasks and heat-softened glass. Though the flame from the bunsen burner was the first time I had ever seen gas, let alone known or used, much less lit it! (Except of course for the carbide bicycle lamp).

It was that winter when Mum decided to take the *Bournvita* advertisement at its word. The first time she bought it for bedtime drinks we were convinced we would not feel cold next day. It was during I believe a History lesson in one of the rooms in the pavilion next the tennis courts that, looking over the frost white grass, I forced myself to resist rubbing goosepimpled arms through blouse and woolly sleeves, by telling myself I COULD not be cold because I had had Bournvita last night!

I found no more aptitude for netball at Wellington than I had for rounders or relay races at Donnington. I failed miserably to grip the hanging rope with plimsoled feet and couldn't climb it one inch. I did my best to please the Gym and Games mistress with bunny-jumps over the low wooden form, the one thing I felt I could do reasonably well, but the only remark I drew forth on the end of term report under that subject was - "Posture needs improvement".

A strange and new experience was that I fell deeply in love, with two girls several years ahead of me. One fair, the other dark, both were tall and lean (I was still dumpy). Both had an air of confidence, and what seemed to me a healthily casual attitude to things. Both were occasionally in trouble. I would have done anything in the world to please either of them, but neither knew, nor did anybody else. Jean and Freda, I've long forgotten their surnames.

Something of Headmistress Ross's reputation for strictness shewed from time to time, like when another older girl was held as an example during school assembly. Miss Ross explained that on this occasion the girl was not, after all, to be expelled, but we were warned that anyone else might not be so spared. And what had that poor and dreadful girl done? She had removed her eyebrows - and drawn them in again with pencil lines!

Once I had some reason to go down the stately staircase during lesson time, when all was quiet, on my own. My hands were enjoying the feel of the polished wood of the banister under them as I moved. Round the last turning I met Miss Ross.

"Are you ill, child?"

"No, Miss Ross."

"Then do NOT hold the bannister. Walk properly with your hands to your sides. Carry yourself with your muscles!"

The truth about having to move from Uckington dawned one Saturday when Dad and Mum and I went into Shrewsbury by bus – then caught another, Bunce's bus to the end of Oak Lane at Bowbrook. We walked down the lane, over the little wooden bridge over the brook, to the first of two cottages on the left, Number Two Oak Cottages. The Onions family lived there. Mr Jack Onions was Dad's Ploughing Match friend. The reason for our visit was that Mr Onions was moving to another farm, and Dad had applied for his job as waggoner at Oak Farm, for Captain Clapham of Bowbrook House. There was a bright fire and the kitchen smelt as though they had had roast meat for dinner. (It never lost the smell - ever - all the years we lived there).

Having settled the matter of Dad's job and the house and moving day at the end of March, the matter of school was still to be organised.

"She'll have to be transferred to the Priory," Dad said.

Now, whether my parents' view of the procedure was altogether too simple I will never know, but Miss Ross did not see it as a matter of course at all. Following Mum's letter to her I was summoned to her room.

"Why do you wish to leave this school?" she demanded. It was obvious to me.

"Because we've got to move to Bowbrook, and it is too far for me to come, Miss Ross."

"Why have you GOT to move? Why did you come to this school in the first place?"

It took a lot of explaining that because the farmer was moving from Uckington and another farmer coming, all of the old families had to move because the cottages went with the farm. In the end she was exasperated.

"Go, then!" she commanded – "And I'm glad to be rid of you!"

I had not expected that, and I knew she was not really glad, because, for all my faults I was a good scholar and attended and behaved more or less as I should. She could not understand the pattern of events.

And we all did move. When father turned, so to speak, we all turned. The farm family with my special Joan, Barbara and George moved to Booley, near Stanton-on-Hine-Heath. The Taylors with my friend Hilda, went to Smethcott. The last time I saw Hilda after a visit, she waved from a cottage doorway just beyond Smethcott Woods. Luthers, I believe, went somewhere Wellington direction. The Beedles family with Joanie and Reggie went to a farm of their own called Criftins, near Upton Magna. I don't remember where the others went.

And after all those years at Donnington, I was to join my third school within less than twelve months. I ought to be able to tell more about actually leaving Uckington itself, but memory is here proved to be selective. I don't remember saying goodbye to anybody, even my closest friends, or about leaving the lanes and the fields and all those special dreaming-places. Probably I had not really believed that they were not, by some magic or other, coming with me.

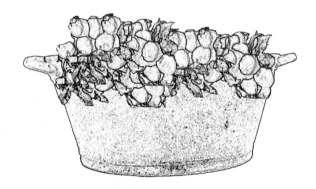

Shrewsbury ?

• BUCKINGTON

WELLINGTON
→ 5

WHEATHILL

UPPINGTON

THE WREKIN

NORTON

WROXER

ETTON-ON-SEVERN

Beacon

DONNINGTON

Charlton Hill

Wem Baptist Church
Ladies Outing to Grinshill

Back Row: Miss Edie Williams (?) Mrs Ryder Miss Ede Farlow   Mrs
              Davies (Barker's Green) Mary Farlow (wife of Harry Farlow)
              Miss Annie Farlow ('Nance')
Middle Row: Mrs Stanley Edge   Mrs Arger Selina Farlow (granma – also
              known as Lena) Mrs Tom Edge Miss Alice Farlow ('Auntie
              Alice')
Front Row: Doris Farlow (daughter of Mary and Harry above)

Donnington School 1937

Front row,
from left: Reg Carter Eric Dorsett Brian Teece Joan Egerton
              Joan Carter Bob the spaniel Sybil Egerton Pamela Coggins
              Betty Smith holding Jock the terrier   Joan Beedles John
              Davis Ted Butler Len Rogers

Second row,
from left: Betty Shore June Shore Rose Starling Olwen Davis
              Edie Hughson

Third row,
from left: Reg Beedles Alwen Davies George Ryley Frank Fowkes
              John Carter Reg Jones Alf Naggington Bill Parry
              Don Harding John Pritchard John Churms Ritch Churms

Fourth row,
from left: Connie Pritchard Betty Parry Marion Morris Gwen Leake
              Betty Mainwearing Gladys Taylor Barbara Ryley Selina
              Farlow Vera Starling Dot Blount Barbara Lewis

Top row,
from left: Pat Morris Jim Harding Arthur Noakes Harold Williams
              Bill Harding Frank Carter

CURRENT PUBLICATIONS

Yours Reverently
From *The Parish Notes* 1948-1953 by REV.WILLMOTT
ISBN 0953180204

The Parson Knows
From *The Parish Notes* 1953-1968 by REV.WILLMOTT
ISBN 0953180212

The Vicar Calls
From *The Parish Notes* 1968-1982 by REV.WILLMOTT
ISBN 095318028X
£9.99 each (£11 p+p) £25 the trilogy (inc. p+p)

Greening – A family surname over 500 years
Family History by MICHAEL GREENING
ISBN 0953180220
£9.99 (£11.0 inc. p+p)

Admiring the View
Poems by KEVIN BAMFORD
ISBN 0953180255

Heavy on the Tree
Poems by BRENDA WHINCUP
ISBN 0953180239

Makings
Poems by JUSTINIAN
ISBN 0953180271

More Makings
Poems by Justinian
ISBN 0954305302

Severn to the Dee
A railway book by the SHROPSHIRE RAILWAY SOCIETY

Women who knew Jesus
A New Testament re-telling by JEAN MCCARTNEY
ISBN 0953180298
£4.95 each (£6.0 inc. p+p)

Demon in the Bottle
A factional story about Billy the River Severn alcoholic,
and Bungus the last coracle-maker by STEVE FOX
ISBN 0954305302
£3.75 (£5 inc.p+p)